To Jerry, Mary & Douglas –

Hope you decide to try more of the
shell game! Best

Murray Hoyt

JEWELS FROM THE OCEAN DEEP

THE COMPLETE GUIDE TO SHELL COLLECTING

JEWELS FROM
THE
OCEAN DEEP

THE COMPLETE GUIDE
TO SHELL COLLECTING

By Murray Hoyt

G. P. PUTNAM'S SONS
New York

To the shell collectors I have known, the most ener-getic, competitive, individualistic, tolerant, interest-ing and thoroughly delightful group of people in the world, this book is affectionately dedicated.

Photographs 2, 4, 5, 6, 7, 18, 23, 28, 32, 33, 37, 38, 39, 42, 44, 47, 51, 52, 53, 54, 55, 56, 57, 58, 59, 64, 65, 66, 67, 68, 69 were taken by Alice Denison Barlow of shells in her own collec-tion; photograph 8, courtesy of the American Museum of Natural History.

Copyright © 1967 by Murray Hoyt

Library of Congress Catalog

Card Number: 67-20439

PRINTED IN THE UNITED STATES OF AMERICA

Acknowledgments

A great many people have helped me with this book in a great many ways. If I listed them all, each with his contribution to the overall effort, I'm afraid the publishers would have to jack up the price of the book to cover the cost of extra paper and typesetting. So perhaps I had best confine myself to a few, plus a blanket "thank-you," heart-felt, for the others. I assure them that their help is both remembered and much appreciated.

First, my thanks to Mr. Ben Rogers of the Rogers Photo Service in Middlebury, Vermont, for his patience and skill in taking many of the pictures herein, and for developing or printing many of the others.

And to *Reader's Digest* magazine, Mr. Ben Hibbs, Mr. Ken Stuart and Mr. John Wells for their permission to use on the jacket the color transparencies by J. D. Barnell from my May 1965 article in their magazine. To Mr. Barnell especially, for producing such fine work.

To Miss Edith Mugridge of the Glory-of-the-Sea shell shop on Sanibel Island for a dozen pictures of her shells, including the famous Glory-of-the-Seas Cone. To Jo and Jim Pickens and to Bill Burpee for their pictures and help. To Alice Denison Barlow for photographs she took of many shells in her own collection.

To the officers and the personnel of the Bixby Memorial Library in Vergennes, Vermont, for permission to photograph shells from the Rosa Agnes Wilke collection. To Mr. and Mrs. Eben Joy, owners of the famous Vermont eating place, the Dog Team Tavern, for making their shells available to me; to the D. D. Butterfields for the use of their shells.

To R. Tucker Abbott, Pilsbry Chair of Malacology, Academy of Natural Sciences, Philadelphia, for his help with the original *Reader's Digest* article which triggered this book.

To the various people who furnished props for picture-taking and especially the brothers Cheng of Guy Cheng Gifts, Charlotte, Vermont. (Older readers will remember Guy Cheng as Chinese Davis Cup captain back in the Don Budge era.)

To Mrs. Lawrence Zern for typing the polishing copy and the final from some pretty badly hacked-up manuscript.

And finally to Marg Hoyt, my wife, for recipes, for proofreading and for all-around companionship.

To all of you, and to all the others, thanks!

Contents

8 *Contents*

Introduction

Shell gathering is like eating peanuts. It doesn't take much to get you started, and once started you have difficulty stopping.

I myself am a classic case in point. Twenty-some years ago I went to Sanibel Island off the west coast of Florida, one of the great shell-gathering areas of the world, to write a book. I wanted quiet in lovely surroundings, with sunning and swimming and fishing for recreation after work. Above all I did *not* want shells. Never would I pick up even one shell, I assured all those who mentioned how lucky I would be to have so many fine shells right in my front yard.

I had been there about a week when my wife, Marg, and I came across a murder mystery serialized in the old *Collier's* magazine. It was by Richard Powell, and was called "Shell Game." The scene was a fictitious area which nicely combined Sanibel Island and Fort Myers Beach. The plot and its solution hinged on shells. Shells found in a certain area were where they should be as far as the non-shell gatherers were concerned. But to the hero, these shells were the clue, the turning point. Some should never have been where they were. Some should have had a protective covering, or parts of one, on the outside of the shell. Some should have had barnacles and other encrustments or stains on them. But these shells had all been lovingly cleaned and even polished. That fact finally landed the murderer in jail.

Here we read about Angel Wings, and the next afternoon, walking on the beach after work, I was startled to see a shell I knew must be an Angel Wing. I had never seen one or even read a description. But the shell looked so much like the wing of an angel that I knew it must be that shell. I picked it up; I would pick up only this one, but I had to show Marg.

We read about a Cat's Paw. The next day I saw one. I *knew* it must be that, it looked so much like it. I picked that up, too. We read about Turkey Wings, Scotch Bonnets, Lady's Ears, and many others. The next day or the day after or the day after that, I'd find them on the beach and pick them up. Nobody pointed them out to me; nobody had to.

Naturally I spotted some I didn't recognize. And there were others I read about but didn't find. So I started looking for these. And I was hooked. Firmly, irrevocably I was hooked. Many years and a reasonably large collection later, I'm still hooked. Unlike a fish on a line I found it painless —downright enjoyable, in fact—extremely interesting, and most challenging. And I never even struggled.

In shell gathering, one thing leads to another. I couldn't find a King's Crown Conch with sharp points on the open beach and somebody suggested I go to the shallow water on the bay side of the island and get one live. I did so, with spectacularly fine results. I progressed from one area of shell gathering to another in this way.

I looked for a book that would, so to speak, take me by the hand and lead me through progressive stages as I came to them. At that time I could not find the type of book I wanted. The books I did find were fine books. Their authors were scientists and probably couldn't conceive of *any* person knowing as little about shells and shell gathering as I knew. Anybody, that is, who still was interested enough to buy a book about it. The shell names were all in Latin, and I wasn't ready for this. I had no idea, for instance, that *Barnea costata Linné*, which I heard an expert discussing, was actually the Angel Wing I had found first. The beginner must have the need for Latin names explained to him; he must be convinced. Then he must have the naming explained before he will understand or get much good from them.

I needed to know about the animals that lived in the shells, what the shells were made of, how the making was done. I wanted to find out the feeding habits of the animals and where, while feeding, they could be found. I wanted to learn as many as possible of the interesting facts which had been discovered through the ages about any and all of them.

I wanted to know about the people who collected shells and how I could successfully become one of them. I was positive that there was a great wealth of fascinating information that the scientists seemed to assume everybody knew. I didn't, and I wanted to. If I could find out these and similar facts, they would form a solid base on which I could build my new hobby.

I never found such a book at the start of my collecting. I did, however, find the wealth of fascinating fact which I had been sure was there for anyone who liked to learn about Nature. I found it by asking questions, by reading, by trial and error.

This book, then, is my effort to provide the beginner with the book I was looking for when I was first exposed to shells. The facts I have picked are, I fondly hope, interesting facts. I have tried to tell them for the layman, the nonscientist. They are the essential facts, the facts you'll need at each stage to enjoy your hobby to the utmost and to lead you on to more sophisticated study and collection. Through this book you will be made ready for the identity catalogs and the extremely advanced scientific books on malacology and conchology.

In this book I have paralleled the course of my own gradual shell sophistication. The book should, therefore, be helpful to any shell collector at any stage in his education, clear up to highly scientific specialization.

With it, and guided by it, I wish you fun, adventure, knowledge and health.

MURRAY HOYT

1

Shell Gathering

S HELL gathering is a hobby enjoyed by millions; by rich, by poor, by in between.

It can be as expensive or as inexpensive a hobby as you want to make it. If you gather the shells yourself it costs you nothing. The shells lie there on the ocean beaches of the world, sometimes in huge windrows, sometimes widely scattered. There are billions more of them than all the shell collectors in the world could pick up. You only have to decide which, from the great collectors' feast, you want to keep. It's as simple as that. Space, specimens already picked up, conditions of the specimens, numbers of them available—all these influence your decision. What other hobby can be that inexpensive? You just pick up what you want and nobody says no to you.

The animals wearing these shells exist in vast numbers on tidal flats, in the ocean's depths, along its edges. They, too, are free. All you have to do is catch them, dig them, or whatever, and again your only decision is which ones you want to keep.

If you want to pick up extras of shells that for some reason are at some particular time plentiful in your area, and you want to trade your good excess with other shellers throughout the world, the financial outlay can still be negligible.

But if you go into the market and bid for rare shells to

fill out blank areas of your collection, up to and including a Glory-of-the-Seas-Cone, a Great Spotted Cowrie or a Prince Cowrie, your outlay could cause even the directors of the Ford Foundation to wince.

It is a fascinating hobby. The shapes of these calcium creations are interesting, graceful, and almost as varied and numerous as the collection of fingerprints in the F.B.I. archives. Some are heavy, rugged, strong. Some are so fragile you wonder how they ever came through the surf and landed on the beach unbroken. Their colors are almost as varied as their shapes. A sieveful of Coquinas, tiny clams, will present enough color combinations and color designs to keep a cloth manufacturer busy for years. The scallop family is vastly colorful.

The animals which make and inhabit these shells live interesting, unique lives. Some spend a wild, untrammeled youth swimming about freely, then attach themselves to something solid and remain there till they die. Some retain the same general contours from birth to death.

Some shell inhabitants eat other shell inhabitants. Their methods of doing so vary widely, from boring a hole through the victim's shell to prying the shell open. A starfish even extrudes his own stomach inside the shell of the oyster he has opened, digests the inhabitant inside its own home, and then draws back his stomach within himself. Some shell inhabitants escape their enemies by digging deep in sand or mud, some by leaping with their foot, and some, believe it or not, swim away by snapping together the two parts of their shell to force out water—a sort of jet propulsion.

Most of the shell-wearers have the amazing ability to produce a calcium secretion with which they enlarge their quarters, repair them, and even cover a bit of foreign matter that gets inside those quarters and hurts them, thus forming a pearl. I use the word "most" because sometimes you see a definitely inhabited shell moving along the sand. And upon investigating you find that a hermit crab has appropriated an unused shell and is living in it.

Shell gathering can be a hobby as gentle as two little old ladies having the minister's wife over for tea. Or it can be as dangerous for the ignorant or the adventuresome as hunting lions or tigers without a gun.

The animals that inhabit some of these shells have a sting as deadly as a rattlesnake's. Too, the stingray, which a sheller wading in roily water might step upon, could whip a stinger around and into a leg or ankle, injecting a possibly lethal dose of poison. A sea urchin has spines that will pierce the rubber sole of a sneaker and inflict a painful wound. Barnacles have edges as sharp as the stainless-steel blades advertised so lyrically on television; anything that stays long under salt water can become barnacle-covered so that without know-how a careless hand can be badly cut by the end of the shelling day.

There are fearsome items like the Moray Eel and the Giant Squid with which a sheller, skin diving for specimens, can come face to face. There are noxious odors. There is acute sunburn, which can leave the foolhardy sick and tortured, unable to stand even a sheet against their raw flesh. There are many other dangers. It is one purpose of this book to tell the shell gatherer what precautions to take and what equipment to use so that he may shell safely even in dangerous areas.

In time spent, the hobby of shell gathering can be anything from a one-day-a-year beach trip to an all-consuming passion that fills a student's vacation or the empty hours of the newly retired individual.

Even the one-day-a-year beach trip gets all the family out in the open. There is fun and exercise and something to carry home to show to friends.

To others, though, shell gathering becomes a way of life. And, I'm convinced after watching for many years, a good one. The real addict walks miles, tans a deep brown, spends hours on the beach in the fresh air, bends over again and again, to the everlasting benefit of his waistline. There was a retired woman doctor in her seventies whom I saw almost every morning with her little basket. She broke her hip a-while back. Just as soon as she could bear her weight on it she was back at shell gathering; she could hardly wait. She could no longer wade or swim. But every day she walked with her cane, increasing the number of hours slowly, in the morning and again in the afternoon, looking for shells. And the hip grew constantly stronger.

This mild exercise is good for almost everyone except heart cases, and especially good for older people. As collectors, older people are not just sitting in a chair, waiting. They're alert, busy, interested, learning, happy. They find a coveted specimen and there are hours of excruciating triumph. Their off-the-beach hours are filled with cleaning, cataloging.

Shell gathering transports the collector of any age mentally, sometimes even physically, to far romantic places. He learns more about geography and marine biology than school ever taught him.

It is, in my opinion, infinitely more interesting, instructive and demanding than, for instance, coin collecting or stamp collecting. Before the proponents of these hobbies can protest, I hasten to explain.

There is, by and large, little or no physical effort connected with coin or stamp collecting: no walking, wading, digging, swimming, diving. The shuffling of pages, the lifting of coins, the pasting of stamps would be about it, physically. There would be no pulling all day on a rope attached to a heavy dredge, no lugging a boat or canoe overland to some secluded inlet. A shell gatherer, even an ancient and relatively inactive shell gatherer, will get plenty of exercise.

There is, too, the matter of knowledge gained. Admittedly there is a lot to learn about other hobbies. But the deeper you delve, the more specialized coin or stamp information you get. The more you delve into the world of shells, the more you learn about, and are awed by, the facts and the mysteries of life and propagation. A vast and little-known area of the world around us takes on interesting meaning.

You find yourself learning all sorts of interesting facts not only about shells and their animals but about tides, sunrises, birds, trees, stones, aquatic vegetation, currents, acids, bases, and countless other phenomena.

Few people, though, collect shells *because* it is inexpensive, or educational, or healthful. They don't worry about the fact that the hobby is all wound up with man's instinct to possess, to hoard, or with his love of graceful line and arresting color. They collect shells because it is fascinating fun.

That is a good way to approach it to get the most pleasure from it.

2

Easy Shells to Start You Off

IF you take up a hobby for fun, it is nice to be able to start it without going to a school, without needing a whole covey of teachers, even without too much self-teaching. You might not want to spend a whole lot of time learning the hobby before you find out for sure whether or not you are going to enjoy it. You probably would want to start by having fun and learning as you go along.

With shell collecting, you can do this. You can just go out and start picking up shells. Just as I did, you will find that some of them have such interesting shapes, and are so aptly named for those shapes, that with a list of common names you can recognize a lot of the shells immediately.

I'll cover their Latin names later, carefully. Right now you want to begin. In this chapter, then, I'll talk about some of the interestingly shaped shells of America with which almost anyone, even the rankest shell amateur, would have every chance of starting a collection or adding to one already started. And with no more equipment than just that list of common names plus a desire to give it a whirl. Once you try it, you'll be able to go on slowly or rapidly to more sophisticated shell collecting. At least this way you won't be frightened by the amount to be learned and give up without starting.

So let's begin just as I began: with the Angel Wing. This shell is instantly recognizable on the beach just from knowing

1. Angel Wing (*Barnea costata Linné*). Note the tiny ears near the hinge of the opened shells.

what it is commonly called. It couldn't be anything *but* an Angel Wing. It is a lovely, white, fragile shell. You find yourself thinking of it as having been sculpted while the artist held a Biblical picture before him. You find it hard to bring yourself back to the realization that it has been made as a home by a small animal.

Equally as amazing is the Bleeding Tooth. Obviously the animal inside was no humorist. But there it is, a lower jaw in the opening of the shell, with several spaced teeth in it, *and reddish orange blood seeming to flow down from it and stain the jaw.* (*See jacket.*)

This is nothing for which you need imagination. This *is*

2. Turkey Wing (*Arca zebra Swainson*)

a lower jaw with teeth and blood; you'd swear it. I've seen a non-shell collector come back to the shell again and again and eye it with disbelief. Maybe he, too, felt as if some sculptor were having fun with him. But the shell, quite plentiful in waters near Key West, is a delight to find and to own.

And there's the Turkey Wing. This is one of the ark family of shells that are so plentiful. On Sanibel Island, which occasionally has windrows of shells two or three feet deep in places, about fifty percent of the shells are ark shells in various stages of disintegration. (I shall mention Sanibel Island often because, in addition to my having spent so much time there, no other beach in North or South America has the number or the variety of shells that Sanibel has.) The Turkey Wing is a heavy shell; you'll often find it unbroken. It is between two and four inches long, and you'll have no trouble recognizing it—just look for a turkey's wing in calcium. No one will have to name it for you once your eyes pick one out.

Often it has a short, brownish, matted, weedlike material growing on the outside. On beach-worn specimens this growth is gone, and only the hard surface of the shell itself shows. Such an outside growth, called a periostracum, is common to many shells. Some regular ark shells have a black periostracum which looks as if parts of the shell had been dipped in tar. It dries in the sun and chips off leaving the shell's white surface exposed. A Turkey Wing, even with its periostracum intact, still looks like a turkey's wing.

There is a shell called a Baby's Ear, or a Lady's Ear, which is another shell for do-it-yourself recognition. This is a conversation piece whenever you show it to nonshellers. It *is* a tiny, inch-long ear. It is, however, not always easy to find, for two reasons. First, it is small and white among a beachful of predominantly white shells. And in its live state it is encased *inside* its animal instead of outside. It protects the vital organs of an animal that looks like a glob of gelatin.

There is a variation of this same shell on California

beaches south of Monterey. The one on the East Coast is found from Virginia south. One year my wife and I found, in walking Sanibel Island's beach for several winter months, nine of these shells.

We were proud of this accomplishment as we started the trek back to Vermont. We stopped en route at a Nags Head motel on Hatteras Island. In the late afternoon we walked out onto the dark brown sand beach. Lady's Ears lay there just like ark shells at Sanibel. We picked up a double handful with no more effort than the picking. Ever since then we have been quite chastened about being able to pick up a number of them during the winter.

The tiny Cat's Paw shell is easy to pick out even on a beach full of other shells. It is a small shell with radiating ribs that look like the knuckles on a cat's front foot. In spite of occasionally having a lot more ridges than a cat has knuckles, it is still in the recognize-at-first-glance class.

If you find a huge shell (up to four or five inches) which looks like the Cat's Paw, but with bulbous knuckles, this would be a Lion's Paw. These are often red and are very showy shells. They are hard to find on the beaches I have patrolled.

A second shell in the harder-to-find category is the Scotch Bonnet. But if you were confronted with it on the beach you'd be reminded of a rakishly turbaned bagpipe-blower for sure. It is a white shell; some of them have brown markings. Its lines, with the up-tilted angle of the bonnet brim, are very graceful.

There are two other beach finds which you'd know the moment you laid eyes on them; one is the Old Maid's Curl. There is no need to tell you any more about it than its name. It couldn't be anything else. The other is the Razor Clam; this one is a dead ringer for the old-fashioned straight razor, closed.

There are three others not so easy to recognize just from the common name, but which have a fairly reasonable resemblance to the thing they are named for. These are the

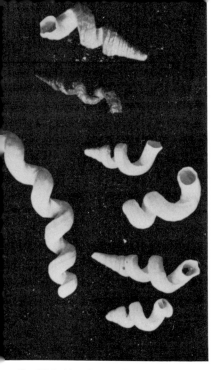

3. Old Maid's Curls (*Vermicularia*), which are made by shipworms.

4. Common West Indian Bubbles (*Bulla occidentalis A. Adams*)

5. Alphabet Cones (*Conus spurius atlanticus Clench*)

6. Boat Shells or Slipper Shells (*Crepidula fornicata Linné* and the spotted *Crepidula maculosa Conrad*)

Bubble, the Auger, and the Drill; you can picture those, and you'd find your picture wasn't far wrong.

In quiet water you'd recognize the tiny Rose Petal just from hearing the name, a tiny little red flower petal. The Chinese Alphabet Cone is another you would surely know. The shape of a cone is known to all of us. When you see a shell with that shape, wide at one end, pointed at the other, it probably belongs to the cone family. Then if you find one with what looks like Chinese writing characters in rows on its surface, that's the shell.

While we're on the subject of the Chinese, the Coolie Hat is just exactly that. You could place one on the head of a tiny Chinese figurine and it would seem to have been designed for the purpose, so perfect is the shape. The shell is a limpet. Some limpets don't look as much like a coolie's hat as others do, but all bear some resemblance.

And finally there's the Boat Shell. This is also called a Slipper Shell. It is shaped like a boat that has a wide seat in one end. There is the slipper resemblance, too, but to me it looks more like a boat. Perhaps this is because I've seen a lot of mullet boats with a huge platformlike seat in back to carry the net. I can almost see a tiny figure standing in the bow of one of these little boats made of calcium, poling it forward, a huge pile of fishnet on the seat.

These are all shells that will interest you just because of their shapes. It would be my hope that if you found some of these it would whet your appetite and make you want to learn more about the animals that made such creations. I'd hope you might want to go on and learn about other shells that perhaps had a less intriguing relationship to their common names, but in their way were just as interesting.

I'd hope that you might want to go on and find out about how the animals make them, and about the history of shells back through the ages. I'd hope that you might want to collect some of these shells and others and study them, and show them to other people and talk about them.

I'd hope, in other words, that it might turn a noncollector into a collector.

3

Mollusks

WHAT about the forming of these interesting shells? They are calcium creations of various shapes, colors and sizes. The animals that make them are called mollusks. Most mollusks live inside their shells as a protection from their many enemies. This protection is desperately needed because the bodies of mollusks are soft. The word "mollusk" is derived from the Latin word *mollis,* meaning soft. A mollusk has no backbone, ribs, or ordinary skeleton as does man, although you might term a mollusk's outside shell its skeleton. This shell, like a human skeleton, remains after the soft body parts have been eaten or have disintegrated following death. Remember that millions of tons of these mollusks' skeletons, in all states of preservation, lie on the ocean bottom or are washed up on the beaches of the world.

Not all mollusks have shells. The soft-bodied squid and the octopus are prime examples of mollusks that don't. Some types of mollusks that do have shells don't have them on the outside of their bodies. I mentioned that the delicate Lady's Ear shell is found inside a glob of soft living material where it protects the vital parts of its mollusk. Some mollusks that do have their shells outside their bodies still don't have shells anywhere near big enough to cover their entire body surfaces. For example, when the Angel Wing mollusk is alive, it does not fit inside the two parts of its lovely shell. It retracts and makes itself as small as it can, but it still cannot cover itself completely.

The Gweduc, or Geoduck, nicknamed "Gooeyduck," which is found along our Pacific Coast, has even less chance of getting completely inside its own shell. Even after its best efforts, it looks a little like a long-faced elephant with its ears plastered forward tight against its head.

There are in the neighborhood of 60,000 species of mollusks. Only the insects of the world can boast greater numbers or diversity. They are found on land (some snails even climb trees), on tidal flats, in rock pools kept filled by spray and tide, in fresh-water lakes and rivers, and in the deep areas of the oceans and seas. I found one reference to the taking of shelled mollusks at the record depth of 3,000 fathoms—just over three miles. At this depth, with such an overwhelming weight upon them, the mollusks are drab and don't appear to move around much. They seem to take their nourishment from the rain of dead matter constantly settling on them from above.

Those that live in tidal areas or in pools seem to be able to live for long periods without water. I have seen Coquinas, washed high up on the beach by a storm, bury themselves in the sand. After they had been untouched by the tides for several days, I dug them up and put them in salt water, and they proved to be very much alive.

Many snail mollusks, when pools dry up or the calamity of extreme drought falls upon a land area, seem able to slow down, even to suspend their bodily functions, almost like the hibernation of mammals. The classic example of this is found in the reports of the British Museum. In 1846 two snails from Egypt were fastened to a mounting and added to the museum's collection. They had been there four years when one of the employees noticed what looked like fresh slime at the mouth of one of them. He unfastened the snails from their mounting's and put them in lukewarm water. The next day, much to everybody's astonishment, one snail came out of its shell and ate a little vegetable matter provided for it. After many days, when it had had time to regain vitality, it began to repair the edge of its shell, which

7. Coquinas (*Donax variabilis Say*)

had been nicked on the trip from Egypt. It is a good thing that this tale is vouched for by the British Museum, with its reputation for veracity beyond reproach; otherwise it would be unbelievable.

8. Coral stocks and a Giant Clam (*Tridacna gigas*)

9. A variety of Chitons

Mollusks vary in size from something that would make the head of a pin look large to the Giant Clam (*Tridacna gigas*), which is big enough and frightening enough to be part of a science-horror movie.

I myself have seen Left-handed Whelks (*Busycon contrarium*) so tiny that I had to use a magnifying glass to distinguish more than a dot. I had torn apart the round, leatherlike section of an egg case, and a dozen or so of these mollusks, which had obviously just hatched, were still suspended in the gelatinlike material inside. The magnifying glass showed that each one was encased in a perfect, unbelievably tiny shell, and looked in every miniature detail exactly like every large Left-handed Whelk that I'd ever seen.

At the other end of the size scale, I've seen Left-handed Whelks a foot long; Horse Conchs (*Pleuroploca gigantia*) twenty-two inches long. But the prize of them all, the shell to end all shells, is that Giant Clam. I've seen Giant Clam shells that measure two feet across, but these were, I judge, young and undeveloped compared with the record four-foot-six-inch specimen, which weighed about a thousand pounds. It had to be moved with rollers and a small army of men. These huge clams are sometimes pretty well hidden in bottom and reef vegetation, and not easy to see. They are said to have drowned pearl divers who carelessly stuck a hand or foot inside the opening between the two parts of their shell. The mollusk clamped shut these halves and the doomed diver could neither pull loose nor lift such a tremendous weight toward the surface. The muscle that holds the two parts together is so strong that they can be pried apart in the really large specimens only with crowbars.

Mollusks are thought to live, on the average, from five to nine years. There are some, however—again the Giant Clam leads the list—that live considerably longer. In some cases, this monster is thought to have lived more than 100 years.

Mollusks are one of the divisions of the animals of the world. Each division is called in Latin a *phylum*. Latin is used in scientific matters not, as the layman probably suspects, just to appear learned and make matters difficult, but to avoid the language barrier between scientists of different countries. Just as written music needs to be common to all languages, so scientific data has to be described in a way which will mean the same thing to a Frenchman, a German, an Italian or an Englishman.

Mollusks are *mollusca* in Latin. Phylum mollusca, then, is divided into five classes: the crepipods (*Crepipoda*), the scaphopods (*Scaphopoda*), the cephalopods (*Cephalopoda*), the pelecypods (*Pelecypoda*), gastropods (*Gastropoda*).

Don't let that paragraph frighten you into giving up all thought of collecting shells. Three of these classes we'll deal with only in passing. And the other two—the pelecypods and the gastropods—which will be dealt with thoroughly throughout the remainder of this book, have easy-to-remember common names which you can use until the Latin becomes easy for you.

The crepipods are a small class of mollusks. Their shells are made up of sections which, along with the strong leatherlike material which binds them together, overlap like fancy, pointed shingles on a house. There are eight of these sections.

These mollusks are commonly called chitons. When you are looking for chitons you search among rocks. You look underneath the rocks, in crevices between them, or wherever there is a hiding place. The only place you don't look is out in the open. Rocky headlands or tidal rocks would prove to be productive. There are approximately 150 species of chitons, and they are found along both the Atlantic and Pacific coasts. There are variations in characteristics, but the eight segments and the leatherlike girdle holding them together are common to practically all of them. Their nickname, coat-of-mail shell, stems from this resemblance to chain-mail armor. About twice as many of these species are found on the Pacific Coast as on the Eastern Seaboard.

The shells of these mollusks are dark and nondescript on the outside, but the underside can have beautiful coloring.

The ones I have come in contact with were a lovely dark blue. Others can be white or cream, or white with pinkish streaks.

What must you as a collector do to add some variations of these shells to your collection? First of all, when you find the mollusk in his hiding place, use a jackknife blade to loosen his hold on the rock surface. The chiton has a muscular foot with which he moves himself along, and with this he can fasten himself to the rock so firmly that he must be pried loose. But if the knife blade is slid under him suddenly, he can be removed fairly easily. If you don't do it this way you may have to use a chisel and ruin the shell.

Flatten the animal against a small piece of wood before he has a chance to curl into a ball. If he dies while he is curled up, it is next to impossible to flatten out his shell properly. Bind him with string to the flat surface of the wood. Then kill him by dipping wood and all into a strong alcohol solution. Later, when he is dead, you can remove the bindings and scrape out the flesh. This procedure is recommended by Dr. S. Stillman Berry, who knows as much about chiton collecting as any person in America.

Next come the scaphopods, popularly known as tusk shells or tooth shells. The common name stems from their shape. They look like tiny models of elephant tusks that have had their pointed end sawed off. These shells were the wampum used by the Indians of our northwestern states in trading with other Indians. Eastern wampum was made of pieces cut from shells and pierced for stringing. The tusk shells were used whole, and because both ends were open, could be strung without being pierced.

These shells aren't very colorful in temperate areas; mostly they're chalky white. Some, though, are ribbed; some are polished. There are about 100 different varieties, and in the East Indies they boast bright colors, particularly shades of green.

The animals live buried in mud or sand, the small end of the shell about even with the surface of the material they're buried in. At the other end there is a triangular, concave foot and a sheaf of hairlike appendages anchored next to the mouth. These have nubs on the outer end and weave about to capture microscopic organisms for food. If these hairlike appendages are broken off, they grow back. This is why they are often of different lengths.

Tusk shells are found mostly in deep water, but a few live in water shallow enough that the dead shells are washed up on the beaches. They are small, some of them about the size of half a pin. The giant of the whole class is said to be only 4.9 inches in length. There are two families, whose Latin names are far more imposing than the mollusks themselves: *Dentaliidae* and *Siphonodentaliidae*. These, incidentally, are interesting names because they show the prospective shell collector that Latin names aren't always as formidable as he may have feared they would be. A lot of English words are derived from Latin. If you examine the words carefully there's often a clue to the meaning, whether you ever studied Latin or not. In this case our word "dental" jumps out at you in that first name. You know it has something to do with tooth. The tooth shell. The Latin word is *dens*, and the genitive is *dentis*, "pertaining to teeth." In the second name the "dental" part is combined with the word "siphon."

Again applying this principle, when you see the name of one of the species, *Dentalium elephantinum* (this is the green one I spoke of), you can be pretty sure that this shell is one of the largest of the tooth shells. This makes the whole imposing name pretty easy to understand.

If you want some of the tusk shells for your collection, keep your eyes open for them along all our beaches. Some species are found as far north as Nova Scotia. For fine, undamaged specimens, a dredge that digs in a bit is your best bet.

The cephalopods are to me the most interesting of the mollusks. This is because they are the most highly developed —and because some of the members present danger, menace, astounding size, even horror. All these items add up to interest. Something you would be terrified to encounter in its own element is bound to be a lot more interesting than, for instance, an oyster that is attached to a mangrove root, just staying where it is for life.

This class hasn't actually much to do with shell collecting, because only one of them, the Chambered Nautilus, has a real external shell. However, that one is beautiful enough to make up for the shortcomings along this line of the rest of the class.

The squid and the octopus, with no shell, and the cuttlefish, which has an internal shell called a cuttlebone, are part of this class. That internal shell of the cuttlefish has been a great boon to the canary and parakeet business. It is attached to the inside of a cage for imprisoned birds to peck at, as a source of calcium.

These three have in common arms called tentacles. The octopus has eight, the other two have ten each. The tentacles of the octopus and squid have suction cups spaced along the length of each tentacle. These allow the animal to clutch and strangle and hold onto food and foe. These creatures therefore look a bit like the cut-off heads of bald men with staring eyes and long beards in eight or ten braids—a pretty repulsive appearance.

The octopus, in spite of this horrible appearance, is mild, inoffensive and retiring, and likely to be fairly small except up in the neighborhood of Alaska, where one species, which was twenty-seven feet in diameter when its tentacles were all spread out, has been found. The octopus moves in the water, and occasionally even out of it, by a sort of tentacle walk, using the tentacles the way we use legs and feet. But it darts by ejecting water rapidly. It isn't anywhere near as fast in its movements as the squid, which has quite a reputation along that line.

The squid can be large and altogether appalling. The Giant Squid, in fact, has a reputation in literature probably far more fearsome than anything warranted by actual fact. There are stories of these huge mollusks wrapping their tentacles around ships and dragging them under, terrific stories that make exciting movies.

Actually the largest specimen recorded was about eighty-five feet in diameter. This is still a fantastic size, but it just isn't in the ship-dragging-under category. It is, however, plenty big enough to be in the whale-fighting class. Some whales feed almost exclusively on small squid and get into altercations with the big ones to the extent that they have long scars on their sides from the suction cups on the tentacles of these monsters. In the American Museum of Natural History in New York there is a huge model of such a fight.

It can be seen from this that the suction cups get a real hold. They do this in an interesting way. The suction disc comes in contact with a flat surface and the tentacle then retracts the center of the disc, thus creating a vacuum that in turn creates suction or holding power. This holding, multiplied many times—by the number of discs in contact—is something from which even a whale finds it very hard to break away.

The octopus eats shelled mollusks, crustaceans and fish. Often he has a lair in some sort of hole or under a rock overhang. Usually you can tell that such a lair is near by the piles of shells. Sometimes he drags rocks to him with his tentacles and hides himself in a sort of blind.

The squid, on the other hand, is more a free-swimming character and is all mixed up with the fish industry. Cod and mackerel and other kinds of fish, in addition to the whales, think he's delicious. He is therefore netted, cut up and pretty universally used for bait by commercial fishermen.

The mature fish eat small squid, and the squid eat small fish of these same kinds. Each is, therefore, a great force in holding down the population explosion of the other. Schools of squid seek out schools of small mackerel and cod. They have a reputation for lightninglike jet-propulsion spurts accomplished by shooting water out the siphon. They can change course rapidly by changing the angle of the siphon while it ejects water. So when they attack a school of fish, they suddenly spurt into it backward, whip sideways and attempt to get tentacles on a fish. Sometimes they succeed; often they don't.

If they succeed, they instantly bite a three-cornered chunk out of the back of the victim deep enough to sever the spinal cord. The interesting thing is that this three-cornered wound is always in the same place, as if the squid had used a ruler to settle on a spot to make the incision. Carl Lane, author of the standard *The Boatman's Manual,* tells me that in Maine, where he lives, squid attacking schools of fish this way in shallow water sometimes jet-propel themselves up onto the sand and can't get back. They perish by the dozens.

Both the octopus and the squid, because of their ability to dart, are able to take care of themselves nicely. But in addition to that defensive maneuver and their ability to hold and strangle and bite, they have two other methods for confounding attackers. They can discharge an inky substance which not only keeps an attacker from knowing exactly where they are, but which also is thought to have an acidlike effect on the attacker. And squid have a chameleonlike ability to change color and blend in with the area in which they find themselves. They can be dark and spotted, or almost transparent, or many colors in between. Deep-water cephalopods use phosphorescence to help capture prey.

Eons ago these mollusks had shells, some of them tremendous, as fossil remains show. It may have been that these shells retarded locomotion to the point that evolution and the survival of the fittest gradually did away with them.

The Chambered Nautilus and the Paper Nautilus are cephalopods, too. These, too, add to my feeling that this is the most interesting family of them all. There are major differences between these and the octopus, squid and cuttlefish. For that matter, each of these is very different from the other.

We'll take the Paper Nautilus (*Argonauta argo*) first. This is the creature which, through the ages, has appealed to poets. The shell is paper-thin and very lovely, almost weightless. It is shaped a little like a half moon, narrower at one end than the other. Actually it is not a nautilus at all; the make-up of the shell and the use are very different from the Chambered Nautilus (*Nautilus pompilius*), but they look alike superficially. The shape ends the similarity, and malacologists like to have it called an Argonaut Shell.

The shell, which is covered with radiating lines of nodules on the outside, is made by the female only, using the wide membranelike paddles or mantles on two of her tentacles. Being so light and thin, the shell will float, and the mollusk in ancient poetry and allusion was said to get inside, raise the two paddlelike tentacles as sails, steer with the other tentacles hanging over the side like oars, and go venturing off across the sea to far romantic places. This concept persisted for centuries. Aristotle described this sailing, and Pliny added the bit about the oars.

It's a picturesque concept, but it hasn't much basis in fact. The female uses the shell, when it is finished, as a basket to hold her eggs and later her young. She clutches it to her with the two flattened, membranous, paddlelike tentacles. She has to because she is attached to it in no other way.

She is nearly fifteen times as large as the male of the species. He's the Casper Milquetoast of the mollusk world. Since he has nothing to do with tending the eggs, he has no way of manufacturing a shell and goes through life shell-less. He's seldom over an inch long, which means he's far from imposing. His sex life is slightly on the peculiar side, too. One of his tentacles is modified into a sex organ, is broken off in the mantle area of the female and fertilizes the eggs. Both he and the female move by the cephalopod method of jet propulsion of water through a siphon, and like them the locomotion is backward with the tentacles trailing behind. Sometimes the female floats her beautiful shell egg case on

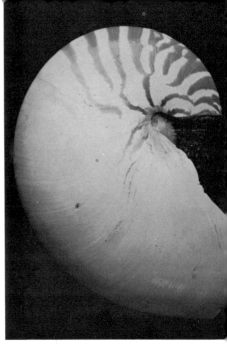

10. Paper Nautilus (*Argonauta argo* Linné)

11. Chambered Nautilus (*Nautilus pompilius* Linné)

the surface; sometimes she doesn't. The *argo* part of the name came from that old sailing myth that I have explained. *Argo* was the name of the ship on which Jason sailed.

The other nautilus, Chambered Nautilus (*Nautilus pompilius*), has the only shell used among the cephalopods the way we have come to expect a shell to be used: as a home for its maker. But even here there is a difference. Many mollusks, as they grow, move along into larger quarters as they enlarge their shells. Some even seal off the abandoned areas. But only in the Chambered Nautilus shell are the chambers sealed off and filled with gas which lightens the heavy shell under water.

The shell itself is heavy and when cleaned has a lovely, pearly luster. It is brown-striped. When English sailors first saw these shells floating, they thought they were seeing drowned tortoiseshell cats. The inner surface is mother-of-pearl in delicate coloring from the faintest blush of pink to lovely aquamarine.

The animal that lives inside, like the other cephalopods, has tentacles. Mostly it lives in very deep water, and when it is captured at these depths and brought suddenly to the surface, the animal inside becomes the victim of something that resembles the "bends" in humans. This is a malady caused by too quick a trip from heavy-pressure depths to no pressure at the surface. The process of bringing the animal up seems to hurt it badly so that it can not dive again.

The animal, unlike the gastropods, which we will look at shortly and which in some respects it resembles, has no way of sealing off the last and biggest chamber of its shell, the one in which it is living, to protect it from its enemies. They can fairly easily reach in, get hold of it and drag it out. Without the animal inside, the shell will often float on the surface because of the gas in the empty chambers. And thus it is found floating or washed up upon beaches, even though the animal itself is almost never taken alive and healthy.

George Everhard Rumphius, the Dutch naturalist, says that crabs and sharks are the Chambered Nautilus' worst enemies. He says that the young of the species are "not much larger than a Dutch shilling (about one inch in diameter) and are clear mother-of-pearl color within and without." They are usually seen without their outer coating because, of all things, most of the specimens held by collectors have been taken from the stomachs of dolphins and the gastric juices have dissolved those coverings.

There is one more interesting thing about the Chambered Nautilus. It is the only cephalopod fastened to its shell. And this fastening is a cord. It is attached to the soft parts of the animal, and runs back through each of the empty chambers of the shell, clear to the first one. To break this cord and pull out the victim, a crab must anchor one claw to the shell edge, which accounts for the fact that so many of the shells are damaged along the edge.

That, then, is the story of the crepipods, the scaphopods, and the cephalopods, which could be called the "shell-less" shelled mollusks.

4

Mollusk Characteristics

THE gastropods and the pelecypods, the last two classes of mollusks (and the greatest certainly in number), we will discuss in separate chapters. But before we do that, we should examine some of the characteristics which most of these mollusks have in common.

The shelled mollusks, of course with exceptions, have a foot. This is an amazing member. It is used for digging, for locomotion, and for adhering. Many different types of mollusks have come up with other ingenious uses for the foot.

In most cases, in shape it reminds you of a person's tongue. It can, again with plenty of exceptions, be folded like an accordian and drawn inside the shell completely. When it is extended it can be curled and twisted, a great deal the way we stick out and move our tongues. It is a tough, muscular member; it has to be to do some of the things it is called upon to do.

You can best get the picture of a mollusk's digging if you think how you'd use your own tongue in digging a hole in the sand, but with one exception. After the foot burrows down, blood is forced into it to make it big and rigid, which forces aside the sand and makes a hole for the body to be drawn into. This also helps it pull the rest of the mollusk down out of sight into the hole that is thus being wedged out. The Razor Clam, at the same time it is digging in, shoots down a jet of water to help, the way engineers use water when they drive pilings.

I have watched thousands of Coquinas (*Donax variabilis*) digging themselves back down into the sand after they were uncovered at midtide by the wash of the waves. For just an instant these tiny half-inch clams lie there closed. Then, as the wave recedes, out comes the foot from one end of the shell. Almost quicker than I can write it, the foot starts digging in and up-ends the animal. And then rapidly the whole animal disappears from sight before the next wave hits.

Coquinas are sometimes very thick on Florida's surf beaches, though you would never know it to look at the beach. But just wiggle your feet down into the sand at midtide and you'll dislodge dozens, maybe even hundreds of them. None of them will have exactly the same color or brilliant pattern as any other. (This you would guess from that *variabilis*, variable, in the Latin name.) They will be washed down by the receding wave, perhaps be washed back by the next wave. But sometime in the process they will be deposited momentarily on the sand and instantly they will dig in out of sight with that versatile foot.

In the matter of locomotion, the foot is used differently by different mollusks. The most spectacular use of it is made by the Razor Clam, which leaps away from danger with his, using it like a spring. Some mollusks use the foot to pull the whole shell along. In such cases the shell wobbles and hitches along, usually backward, leaving a long mark on the sandy bottom. Many of the snaillike mollusks with a single shell proceed from place to place in this way.

Some of the mollusks have a foot that is particularly adapted to flattening out against some surface, often rock, and creating a suction that defies all ordinary efforts to dislodge the creature. It lies there, usually able to make itself look like a bulging part of the rock itself, safe underneath its shell. The limpets are designed for this sort of foot use. And the abalones of our Pacific Coast, once they're set and ready, can't be dislodged with anything less than a crowbar.

Beside the foot, most mollusks have in common a mantle. This is a most important member, *the* most important as far as the shell collector is concerned. It is the mantle which secretes the calcium carbonate solution with which the mantle builds, adds to, or mends the shell of the animal. Without the mantle there would be no shells to collect!

Mantles are as different in appearance and shape as the shells are different each from the other. On some it is ripple-edged; on some it is brilliant in color. The mantle of the Horse Conch is a gorgeous, almost unbelievable orangey-red. The Queen Conch's is yellow. Some mollusks can extend the mantle out of the opening to cover the entire surface of the shell. The cowries bring it out on each side of the opening, and the two parts creep up each side of the shell till they meet or almost meet on top. With most mollusks, the mantle can be retracted completely inside the shell when danger threatens. And with most, too, the mantle extends all around the rim of the shell.

Few things in Nature are as wonderful as the mantle of mollusks and few things as unfathomable for most of us as its function of shell-building. Take a colorful shell like the Coquina or one of the scallops and examine it. The color patterns are intricate, yet perfect. You wonder at such a multicolored pattern, one that may look like the rays of the sun with each ray drawn out and enlarged at least as regularly as a machine could do it. How can the animal cause its mantle to draw out one color or shade in one line, another different color next to it, a third next to that, all following out the overall sunrise design? Yet it is difficult to find two Coquinas with identical patterns.

You may decide that each section of the mantle produces a calcium secretion of a set color. As the shell grows and the mantle inside grows, the sun-ray color pattern is produced, getting wider toward the rim. But then you spot a Coquina with an oval design and you are hard put to it to fit this one into your theory. Even malacologists argue about some of the details of the operation. Most of the rest of us are content to admire the end result.

If you pick up a murex shell, it will have nubs and spikes

all in a completely regular pattern. How can the mantle create that? Often there are thick spots on the mantle opposite these nubs. One murex, the Pink-nosed Murex (*Murex florifer Reeve*) has a blush-pink tip or apex, the rest of the shell all white. You decide that the mantle of the animal produced pink in its earliest years, white all the rest of the way. You find a shell with a wavy edge fitting tight against the opposite waves of the other half shell, like the Giant Clam. How is this done so beautifully?

Or, the ultimate, you discover a shell that has two rows of spines on a center stalk so long and so thin that they look like and could be the teeth of a comb. The shell is the Venus Comb (*Murex triremus Perry*). How and why does the mantle of that animal produce so spectacular a design? Again, about all a nonscientist can do is admire and marvel.

Most mollusks have in common one or more siphons used for sucking in water, and sometimes food. Many have gills, but not all gills are used for respiration alone as is the case with fish; some are used for catching food particles. Some

12. Queen Conch (*Strombus gigas Linné*)

13. Venus Comb (*Murex triremus Perry*)

14. Two views of the Spider Conch (*Lambis chiragra Linné*)

mollusks have eye stalks on which there are primitive eyes. Carnivorous mollusks, especially, must have some ability to distinguish and attack their prey.

Most mollusks have some sort of mouth, many have a proboscis or snout, and the carnivorous ones have teeth to rasp and shred their food. These teeth are called radula. The number and shape of the teeth in these radula ribbons, or teeth ribbons, are an identification point in telling one subspecies from another.

There are other organs which some mollusks have in common with some others; these we will take up as we come to the particular animals that possess them. But those above are the main ones that most mollusks have and use in common. Of these the mantle, foot, siphon, and the shell itself are the most important for the shell collector to know about.

Mollusks, then, are soft-bodied creatures without a backbone which usually have their skeletons on the outside in the form of shells, but in some cases may have no shell at all. There are five classes of mollusks, one of which is extremely interesting for its way of life, and two others are especially interesting to shell collectors because these two classes produce most of the shells of the world. We will now examine those two, the pelecypods and the gastropods.

5

The Bivalves

PELECYPODS (*Pelecypoda*) have two shells hitched together near the apex, at the opposite edge from the opening, by a hinge and ligament of hard leatherlike material. These ligaments have enough spring action so that when the animal inside the shell is relaxed, or dead, they hold the front of the shell open. In some species, like the pectens, one shell is meant to face down, the other up. The animals will flip over if you place them with the wrong side down. The down side is often less brightly colored.

These two shells, or valves, can open and close like the covers of a book, or like a jewel case. (In fact one shell is called a jewel box.) The parts we have mentioned before, the foot, the siphons, the mantle, can mostly be closed inside these two valves. But we have already noted exceptions to this where the shell was too small to squeeze everything inside. Clams, oysters, scallops, among others, belong to this great class. The name pelecypod means hatchet-footed, and that is exactly what they are.

Pelecypods are popularly known as bivalves. *Bi* denotes two, as in bicycle, and thus a bivalve is a two-valved, or two-shelled, creature. The two valves usually match each other in shape but don't necessarily have to; the two halves of the oyster, and of the fan, which has one flat valve, certainly don't.

The ligament is called the resilium if it is on the inside.

Sometimes there are interlocking teeth that go with the hinge. On many bivalves, on each half near the hinge there is a hump which is called (and looks like) a beak. (Sometimes called an umbo.) This is the spot where the shell started. Usually if the shell is placed on edge with the beak of each half pointing toward you and the top of the beaks up, the end of the shell that is up will be the anterior end

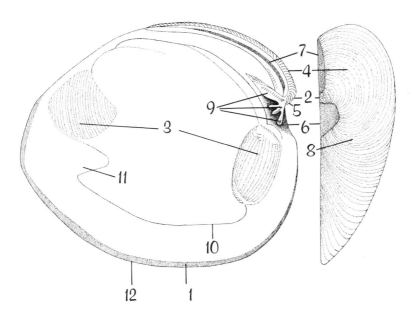

15. Location of the Parts of a Bivalve Shell

1 Lip	8 Periostracum
2 Umbo or beak	9 Hinge teeth
3 Aductor muscle scars	10 Pallial line made by mantle muscle edge
4 Growth rings	
5 Hinge area	11 Pallial sinus (only if species has retractable siphon)
6 Lunule	
7 Ligament and the inside cartilage, called resilium	12 Ventral margin

(The byssus is not present in the Southern Quahog above, but usually when a species has a byssus it radiates from a notch in the ventral margin.)

and the end that is down will be the posterior end. The
anterior will usually be the shorter end of the shell. The
valve on the left side in this position is the left valve, the
one on the right is the right valve.

There is sometimes a depression in front of the beak
called a lunule. Some bivalves that have beaks which don't
point obviously either way, like the scallops or pectens, have
wings called ears sticking out from the hinge area. Some bivalves attach themselves to solid objects with a sheaf of
strong threads called a byssus. And some have that drab-
looking outer covering for their shell, the periostracum.

Bivalves, when danger threatens, usually depend on snapping their two valves together and holding them so tightly
shut that their enemies are foiled. If they can't avoid danger
this way, they usually bury themselves deep to keep out of
danger. The muscle that holds the two valves so tightly together is called the adductor muscle.

The adductor muscle is attached to the inside of each
valve, and on some bivalves you have no trouble finding the
exact spot where the muscle was hitched. There is often a
different color there, or even an indentation in the shell.
The adductor muscle is very strong. Pick up a clam and try
to pry its two shells apart; you can't get your fingernails in
between the two valves, and even if you could you would
break your nails before the valves would part.

Unfortunately enemies of the bivalves have developed
ways of circumventing the holding power of the adductor
muscle. Some wait patiently outside the closed shell until
the animal inside relaxes and opens the valves the slightest
bit. Then the attacker jabs some part of his own body into
the opening.

The King's Crown Conch (*Melongena corona*)—even those
who have never studied Latin know that a corona is a crown
—is one of these. In his case it is his proboscis which he jabs
in. When the shell clamps hard on this, there must be pain
even though the organ is obviously very tough. But the
King's Crown doesn't withdraw when the valves relax a lit-

16. King's Crown Conch (*Melon-gena corona* Gmelin)

tle more; he jams the proboscis in farther. This process is repeated until finally he uses his radula ribbon of teeth to rasp through the adductor muscle so that the valves open and he completes his meal.

Some of the snail-type mollusks pull with the suction of their foot and at the same time pry with the edge of their shell to open a bivalve. The Knobbed Whelk (*Busycon carica*) does this. For anything as clumsy in movement as a shelled mollusk, the Knobbed Whelk displays surprising agility in getting on top of the bivalve he has selected for a meal (often an oyster) in position to bring both the foot and the edge of the shell to bear for prying. He pries the shell open until he can get his proboscis inside and cut the adductor muscle.

The starfish, which is not a mollusk but is more like them than the "fish" in his name would indicate, uses pulling power, only he uses it on both valves since he has five or more arms with suction cups on them. And he has added a diabolical innovation. He squirts a mild poison to help subdue his victim.

He envelops the bivalve with his tentacles and sets up pulling power. The adductor muscle, like any other muscle, tires finally after long-continued strain. At first it has an easy time holding the shell closed. But the strain remains continuous, relentless. After a long time the muscle finally lets up just a tiny bit. After more time, and with the effects of the poison, it lets up a bit more. And then still more, until the fight is over.

However, the fight doesn't always go against the bivalve. Sometimes the starfish gives up before the bivalve does. One scientist tells about a Yellow Cockle (*Cardium muricatum*) which was being attacked by a starfish that suddenly opened its valves, clamped onto a tentacle and broke it off. The starfish, not about to risk the loss of further tentacles, let go and moved away.

Other mollusks, birds, fish, mammals, which find bivalves very tasty, have different ways of getting at them and eating them. The fish that live on shelled mollusks mostly have heavy pincerlike teeth with which they crush small shells. After digesting the mollusk inside, the fish evacuates the pieces of broken shell. Some birds handle the matter in exactly this same way. Other beach birds somehow get their bills inside little bivalves like the Coquina and remove the animal and leave the opened shell.

Man has invented the oyster knife and the scallop knife. All of us have eaten oysters and scallops. For each oyster we or anyone else ate, a shelled mollusk had to be opened and the adductor muscle ripped from the shell on each side. Fortunately, for every scallop anybody ate a bivalve didn't necessarily have to be opened. It is an unpleasant fact of gastronomic life that many of the round items sold as scallops are in reality round pieces of flesh cut from the flippers of the skate.

Excepting oysters, scallops, various clams, and big conchs, most of the other bivalves killed and eaten are eaten by snail-type mollusks. Besides the various effective methods for forcing open the valves that different carnivorous mollusks have, some have an even more direct method of getting a meal of bivalve. They climb upon the bivalve's closed shell and rasp away with their radula ribbon of teeth until they have made a hole in the shell. Some scientists say they secrete an acid to soften the spot, others say no. Through this hole the attacker either feasts on the succulent animal inside by sucking, or kills it or renders its adductor muscle inoperative, and then feeds on it through the main opening.

Bivalves that are fastened to something for life, such as the oyster, have no way of avoiding their enemies. None of them, that is, except the Mangrove Oyster of Florida and West Indian areas. This bivalve has literally climbed a tree to avoid some of its enemies, particularly the snail-type mollusks that crawl along the bottom and bore holes through the oyster's uppermost valve.

Mangroves are bushlike trees which grow at the edge of, or just in, quiet tide water. These bushes put down finger-like prop roots that often do not reach the bottom. These are an inch or so in diameter, smooth and without twigs or small branches. They just hang there in the water at high tide, and partially out of it at low tide. Oysters adhere to the branches and to each other until some mangrove branches I have seen are over a foot in diameter, about eleven inches of which consists of oysters or dead oyster shell. Thus the oyster gets a nice flow of water at medium to high tide, yet is hanging off the bottom out of harm's way from crawling predators.

Incidentally, when fishing in uncontaminated areas, I have chopped off these prop roots covered with oysters, built a fire and roasted them right there on the root, turning them by turning the out-of-water end of the root in my hands. The heat of the roasting opens the shell. All you have to do is take out and eat the cooked oysters and they are delicious.

Other stationary bivalves, though, must put all their hopes in their tightly closed shells. Unlike these, many of the scallops, or pectens, can swim. It's an erratic, jerky sort of swim-

17. Calico Scallops (*Aequipecten gibbus Linné*). Note how much more colorful the upper valve is than the lower.

18. Jackknife Clam (*Ensis directus Conrad*)

ming, but it gets them away from their slow-moving single-valved mollusk enemies. They are sometimes called the butterflies of the sea because of their jerky locomotion and their varied coloring.

They swim by opening their valves and then snapping them closed very rapidly. This forces out water and shoots them along. But it doesn't shoot them backward as you would expect. It shoots them forward as the water is shot out next to the hinges. The File Clam (*Lima lima*) also has this ability to swim. But while the scallop swims horizontal to the bottom, the File Clam swims upright or vertical to the bottom. The File Clam has tentacles which cannot be completely retracted inside the shell when it is closed. These keep the whole animal floating suspended while the valves are being opened so they can be snapped shut again for more propulsion. The scallops don't have anything to keep gravity from working while the valves are taking another bite of water, so their course would naturally be wavering.

If the Razor Clam or Jackknife Clam (*Ensis directus*) is somehow dug out of its hiding place in the sand, on rare occasions it will swim for its life. The Razor Clam moves backward. It pumps along by extending and pulling back that big foot, forcing water out of its shell.

Of all the bivalves, the pectens are the top swimmers. They even swim together like schools of fish, moving from place to place. They can regulate the amount of water which they are forcing out beside their hinge, and in this way steer themselves. A large number of these pectens fluttering along through the water make the viewer who is lucky enough to see them rub his eyes.

Some pectens carry their leaping to incredible lengths. In the book *Fauna of Greenland* by Fabricius, the author says that a northern pecten (*Pecten islandicus*) is much prized by natives as food. But they have trouble cooking it because when they drop it into a pot of water, it jet-propels itself right out of the pot again.

Besides burrowing in sand or mud, and jet-propulsion

swimming, bivalves burrow in other material to hide from their enemies and provide themselves a living area. The most spectacular example and the one that affects man most is the Teredo Clam or shipworm (*Teredo navalis*). This bivalve bores its way into wood that it can reach from under water; pilings, ship bottoms, any kind of wood at all. Nowadays ships are made of steel. But back when there were wooden sailing vessels, the damage to these was terrific. And today pilings are so riddled by shipworms that wharfs and the buildings on them sometimes collapse.

The shipworm has two valves at the front end of its body, and these it rotates in such a way that the sharp-toothed edges dig into the wood. As it progresses farther into the wood and as it grows, the hole it leaves gets larger. Some holes have been discovered as much as a yard long and two inches in diameter. It wouldn't take many of this size to render a piling or a ship bottom pretty flimsy. Often a piling can be honeycombed by shipworms and still show almost nothing on the outside.

As the shipworm digs in, it leaves behind a tubelike lining to the hole it has dug. This hardens and remains long after the worm is dead. One type of shipworm (*Bankia*) is able to plug up the opening of its hole when it senses danger from a change in salt content of the water, or when enemies threaten. The rest of the time it receives a supply of water by unplugging the hole and extending its siphon. The matter of salt content of the water was the only defense which a shipowner had against the shipworm in the old days. If he could get his ship into fresh water, the shipworms and barnacles would be killed. Ships passing through the Panama Canal must go through Gatun Lake, a body of fresh water. How many shipworms and barnacles have been killed in Gatun Lake there is no way of knowing, but the number is legion.

Other bivalves bore into hard clay, into corals and even into soft rock. It takes months and years of work and much renewing of the cutting edges of the shell throughout that time for a mollusk to bore its way into solid rock.

For the most part the bivalves have no eyes. But the scallops are an exception. They have eyes with all the normal eye parts, and they have a whole lot of them. The eyes are along the edge of the mantle next to the opening of the valves, a whole line of them looking like tiny jewels. Those of the bivalves that have a free swimming period before they change into their final form need and have regular eyes at that time so that they can see where they are going. But in the adult bivalves these eyes disappear, except in the scallops. And even with them, some scientists believe that they can do little more than distinguish light and dark and perhaps movement.

Eating and propagation, after self-preservation, are the two most important procedures in the life of a mollusk. The bivalves mostly get their food in one of two ways: They take in water and strain microscopic floating plants and single-celled microscopic animals from it, or they suck in particles of food out of the mud and sand of the bottom through their siphons. This second type usually have longer siphons than the water feeders. The latter sometimes have no siphon at all, but take in the water through a slit in the mantle.

The bivalves that are hitched to something, like the oysters, obviously have to have food brought to them; they can't go to it. The only way it can be brought is on water currents. In the body cavity this water crosses the gills, and mucus on them catches the food and with it is transported to the mouth. Mucus is constantly being manufactured to replace what is used up in this way, much like our saliva. A very large oyster will filter as much water in a year as a railroad tank car would hold.

Bivalves spend varying amounts of their day feeding, but usually it is a lot, possibly as much as two-thirds of each day. In winter, though, when water temperatures are down toward the freezing point, animation seems to be suspended and the bivalves do not feed. The Giant Clam has refined this matter of feeding on one-celled plants far beyond any of the others. It grows its own.

It has a little garden much like a suburbia dweller who owns plenty of land. But the garden is grown on the mantle of the huge clam, and the valves are kept open for the necessary sunshine. On the mantle these plants grow, and excess plant cells are assimilated by the blood cells of the clam. This is one of the most amazing setups in all Nature. The clam can and does eat in other ways, and so is not dependent on its garden. *But these one-celled plants cannot exist without a Giant Clam to grow on,* thus making them completely dependent on their host, or grower.

In the matter of propagation most bivalves discharge eggs or sperm into the water. Some are just male or just female, and discharge just eggs or just sperm. But others have both organs and discharge both. However, in most cases they don't fertilize their own eggs; if they are going to discharge both eggs and sperm, the sperm is discharged first.

Some bivalves start out as one sex and later change. Probably this is not done from an inquisitive desire to try everything. Some bivalves don't discharge the eggs, but hold them in their mantles where they are fertilized by sperm taken into the body cavity with water used for breathing and eating. A bivalve with such a do-it-yourself approach to the matter usually produces far fewer eggs than a bivalve such as the oyster, which broadcasts them. The number of eggs that these broadcasting types of bivalves produce is unbelievable. C. R. Elsey, who has done considerable work in this field, states that one female oyster of a type found on our Pacific Coast and in Japan (*Crassostrea gigas*) will discharge 1,000,000,000,000,000,000,000,000 eggs into the water in one year. Obviously if all the eggs from all the individual females of this bivalve reached maturity, there wouldn't be any room for the rest of us.

Often bivalve eggs that are discharged into the water go through a preliminary stage after the eggs hatch, in which

19. Fresh-water clams and (center) snail from Lake Champlain.

they are very different from the bivalve's final shape. In this stage they swim around using feelers or float around on water currents. This is called a pelagic stage.

Lake Champlain, where I spend my summers, has fresh-water clams. The valves of this bivalve are between three and four inches in length, and though they are mostly white on the inside, some of them have a lovely purple tinge. They have a very pronounced periostracum, which dries and peels off when the shell is out in the air and sunlight. Judging from the number of shells you find on the beach, Lake Champlain must have a tremendous number of these bivalves. There would be a lot more if it weren't for the muskrats, which consider them a great delicacy, in fact a leading staple of their diet.

There is, I maintain, nothing in Nature any more jarring than to go out onto a wharf all alone, no creature in sight, and suddenly, as you near the end, to have a muskrat that has been sitting underneath on a crossbar opening and eating a clam squeal and plunge into the water. This is guaranteed to lop about a year off a nervous person's life.

A bivalve, then, is a two-shelled mollusk which may or may not be able to enclose all its parts inside the two valves. Its enemies are legion and it is considered a delicacy by mammals, fish, and by other mollusks. Mostly it lives its life in one place or one very restricted area. But some bivalves can swim.

6

Univalves

THE gastropods are popularly called univalves. The Latin for "one" is *unus*. Thus these are one-valved mollusks. So many of them are snaillike in shape and characteristics that many people call them "the snails." This is the largest of the five classes. The land snails, conchs, whelks, cowries, cones, volutes, rock shells, abalones, and olives are among the members of this class.

The shells produced by univalves are some of the most beautiful, most gracefully formed objects in the world. As a class, overall, the univalves give us far more really lovely shells than any other.

In most cases the univalve shell is formed around a center column called a columella. Imagine a spiral staircase narrow at the top and getting wider and wider toward the bottom. Then imagine the inside of each step fastened to a thick pole and you have the picture.

Each complete trip around the column is called a whorl. The last one, the largest of all, is called the body whorl. If you hold a univalve so that you can look down at the point, or apex, you can follow each whorl with your eyes. The opening at the bottom is the aperture or mouth. The rim of this mouth is called the lip. Usually there is an outer and inner lip, and the inner lip turns out to be part of the columella.

The univalve in most cases starts the shell at the apex and

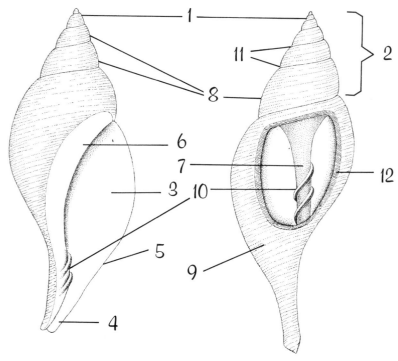

20. Location of the Parts of a Univalve Shell (Dextral)

1	Apex	8	Whorls
2	Spire	9	Body whorl
3	Aperture	10	Columellar ribs or folds
4	Siphonal (Anterior) canal	11	Sutures
5	Outer lip	12	Side of body whorl ground
6	Inner lip (parietal wall)		away to show Columella
7	Columella		

builds it by adding a fast-hardening (even under water) calcium secretion to the edges of the lip with the mantle. Here again, in the univalves the mantle is the shell collector's friend because it is responsible for the size and beauty of the shells, even for the shell itself.

Some apertures are regular in shape, round or oval. But many have a tube or just a notch at the aperture's lower end, and this is called a canal. The ones that look like a tube are sometimes very fancy indeed, even slant up in a graceful, curved line. Some univalves boast two canals, and in this case the upper one is called the posterior canal and the lower one the anterior canal.

Most of the members of this class have a highly developed and versatile foot. In fact the name of the class is derived from a couple of Greek words that mean stomach and foot; thus a stomach- footed mollusk. A horny appendage called an operculum in many of the univalves is attached to the end of this foot. Thus when the animal retracts its foot, the operculum wholly or sometimes only partially closes the aperture and seals the mollusk inside, fairly safe from most of its enemies. *Operculum*, a Latin word, means cover or lid.

The operculums (*opercula*) of different families of shells differ radically each from the other, in shape, size, color and even thickness. Some are shaped like teardrops, sickles, circles, ovals or any other shape that fits.

As for the parts of a univalve inside the shell, this class has, in addition to the parts common to most mollusks, eyes, sometimes on stalks, that give the animals some knowledge of the world around them and tell the carnivorous ones where food is located and how to attack it. They have a head, with mouth, tentacles and a proboscis, and in the mouth the tooth-filled flat ribbon called radula. If the teeth in use become worn down there need be no particular problem. In that case the univalve simply uses more teeth farther along the ribbon.

The siphon usually protrudes through the canal notch, and this siphon is usually retracted when the foot is retracted and the operculum becomes a trap door which seals in the animal.

When the majority of univalves move from place to place, they do so by using their feet. But the ways in which they use them are about as diversified as anything you could imagine. Some of the univalves ripple their huge feet under them and thus ooze along on them. Some can leap with

21. Left-handed Whelks and a small Tulip cut open to show the columella. Below them are several opercula.

22. Captain Cone (*Conus capitaneus Linné*), a handsome univalve

them, and some pull themselves along with them. The Queen Conch (*Strombus gigas*) has a sickle-shaped operculum on a long narrow foot. When the animal starts to travel it sticks out this sickle, hooks it into the sand and pulls itself up to that point. Then it sticks the foot out again, hooks the operculum in and pulls some more. This makes for an efficient, though somewhat jerky, locomotion. Like so many of the univalves, the progress is backward, the apex of the shell pointing toward the rear as the shell bumps along like a pioneer's wagon traversing rough terrain. And of course, the abalones, limpets and others fasten themselves to rocks with their feet in a manner that would make a glue merchant jealous.

In addition to moving on or with the foot, univalves swim,

float, and even dig. They live in trees, on the ground and in both salt and fresh water that ranges in depth from tide pools to the deep, deep areas of the sea.

The univalves are some 80,000 species strong, and the shells of each are distinctive. On some, such as the Florida Cat's Eye (*Polinices duplicatus*), the olives and the cones, the whorls are tiny and the body whorl is tremendous. On others, such as the Screw Shell (*Turritella variegata*), the whorls are very gradually larger all the way down, and the body whorl not much larger than the others. On some, such as the Coolie Hats (*Fissurellae*), there are no visible whorls and there is a hole where the shell should have started at the apex. But this is in the adult shell, and in the early stages of this univalve's life there was a fairly pronounced set of whorls and the hole in the top in the beginning was a slit in the side. (You get the word "fissure" from the name.) This shell is, incidentally, one of the few that has two common names. It is called a Coolie Hat (no name could be more fitting), and it is also called a Keyhole Shell or Keyhole Limpet because the fissure or aperture in its top is the shape of a keyhole.

There is no univalve as large as the bivalve Giant Clam, but the shell with the brassy name, the Horse Conch (*Pleuroploca gigantea*), many times is over two feet long. (There again, with that word "gigantic" staring at you from the Latin name, you'd be pretty sure the shell was no pee-wee.)

At the other end of the size scale there are two or three really small univalves, but the smallest of all seems to be a sand-grain-sized group of mollusks called the Vitrinellas. These you can't see even at my age without magnification. Literally, there is every conceivable size or shape in between.

The univalves breathe with gills, and, unlike in the bivalves, these gills are mostly reserved for breathing alone, not for assimilation of food. Some, like the Coolie Hat, have two sets of gills; it's nice always to carry a spare. Most of them, though, have only the one set.

One of the most interesting facts about the univalves has

23. Six Mandarin's Hats (*Calliostoma euglyptum* A. Adams)

to do with the reproductive process; many of them enclose their eggs in cases which vary in shape as much as the grown univalves do. Most of these cases are so amazing in shape, so large, so different from anything you would normally expect to be deposited by a shelled mollusk, that you almost

24. The egg cases of several mollusks. Top right, mass is attached to an old pen shell.

disbelieve it. That? Come out of a shell? You must be kidding.

There are globs of gelatin full of eggs, gelatin sacs buried, ropes of eggs, collars of eggs, and little discs about the size of a quarter (some larger, some smaller, depending on the size of the univalve that laid them) which are separated each from the other and strung together on a long, tough, fiberlike rope. There are several egg cases that look like morning-glory blossoms all crushed together and held by the stems, there are egg cases in piles, and egg cases that look like little goblets spaced at the stem on a wide ribbon. There are many other shapes and sizes. Two astonishments they have in common: that so big a mass could come from so small a univalve, and that a mass that shape has anything to do with shells.

The most astonishing egg case, as far as I'm concerned, is that string of quarter-sized discs. I once discovered an egg case of the Left-handed Whelk, ripped it apart and found inside in the gelatin little Left-handed Whelks perfect in size and shape that were too small to examine without magnification. This was a unit of one of those long strings of tough-skinned, gelatin-filled, quarter-shaped discs.

Actually nothing on the beach attracts more interest from the casual shell gatherer than these strings of egg cases which are laid by the Left-handed Whelk (*Busycon contrarium*). Tourists will pick the string up, puzzle over it, and try to find out what it is. Then when you tell them, some act angry that you should try to fool people who have asked you a civil question with any such absurd story as *that*.

Actually you can't blame them much, because you probably felt that way yourself the first time you saw one of these. These cases are pale yellowish-brown, and the skin is like tough plastic. The discs may even be the size of a fifty-cent piece at one end, and at the other end may taper down until they are smaller than a dime. They are separated on the stalk, and the stalk is fastened to something solid and laid under the sand at the bottom of the body of water, the discs standing up in a row like a line of on-edge coins. Strings of them are torn loose from their moorings and washed ashore by storms, and that's when shell gatherers come upon them.

Inside there are dots of eggs. If you examine the case at the biggest end of the string and tear it open (which is very, very difficult to do because they are so tough-skinned), you will sometimes find the little whelks formed.

The whole string has a tendency to curl up, but if you stretch it out it can be between two and three feet long. When you realize that a Left-handed Whelk a foot long is a huge whelk, it is no wonder your answer to a beach walker's question is greeted with complete and angry disbelief.

The same is true to a lesser extent with the second most interesting case, the egg collar. This is a huge thing compared with the univalve that manufactures it and lays the eggs. The collar looks as if it had been lost off something big. By no stretch of the imagination does it look like anything that a Moon Shell could have produced. The eggs are spaced inside this collar.

Sometimes in these cases extra eggs are laid, which are called nurse eggs. Their purpose seems to be to furnish food for the hatching univalves. The gelatinlike material in the egg case of the whelk probably contains nourishment, too. The eggs can be laid on the bottom or attached to it. Or they can be laid and protected inside the shell of the female, or they can be discharged into the water to develop there suspended. Some have a different shell in youth from that of their adult life. And some are perfect shells which will simply grow larger.

Incidentally, if you think about the shape of the univalve's shell, you will agree that no other shape except the spiral could have allowed for growth at the lip in the same shape that the animal started out with. It's an extremely simple shape and a simple method of growth. But to my mind there is just no other that could have done the job so efficiently for a one-shelled animal. In this it is like the hexagonal shape that bees pick for their wax cells; no other shape that the finest engineers could come up with would have come so near fitting the larva and at the same time have utilized the space completely. Simple mollusks and insects out-engineer the engineers.

The production of the egg and its fertilization in the univalves is calculated mildly to horrify anyone who judges it by our mammalian standards. Some of the univalves have both sex organs, like some of the bivalves, but mostly they eject the sperm first and through a different duct. Some others are male in their callow youth and female in their staid old age. Some have male organs which shrink and disappear when they reach the female stage of their life. Some exchange sperm with a single member of their own species. Others form a rough ring and exchange sperm around the circle. Some self-fertilize, and scientists have bred close to 100 generations without outside-the-family assistance. Other species are separate in sex, and some of these give no external sign of which sex they are. All these deviations might be looked upon with deep suspicion by a mammal.

The univalves live in the areas where they can find the most of their favorite food. When certain univalves burrow, they do it usually not to hide but to find clams and other burrowing bivalves and to attack and eat them. Usually if you find the King's Crown Conch with his proboscis extended you will find nearby, under the mud, a clam on which he was dining or hoped to dine. Univalves that eat oysters live in shallow water where the oysters live. Univalves that are not carnivorous—and there are many of these —live on, or in, or near, the particular plants they like to eat.

There are several univalves that live inside their dinner. One species lives inside sea urchins, spiny nonmollusks. Another lives inside the flesh of the starfish and just sticks out the end of his shell. Still another lives in the sea cucumber, simply living on whatever the host is living on. No searching for food; it's always there. This life may seem a bit sedentary to a confirmed party-goer, but you've got to admit it's a living.

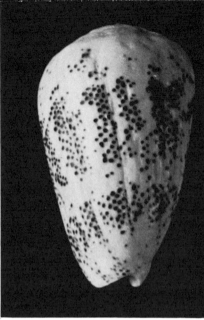

25. A beautiful Silver Conch (*Strombus lentiginosus Linné*)

27. Sand-dusted Cone (*Conus arenatus Hwass*)

26. Three handsome cones left to right, Pacific Lettered Cone (*Conus litteratus Roding*), Prince Cone (*Conus princeps Linné*), Virgin Cone (*Conus virgo Linné*)

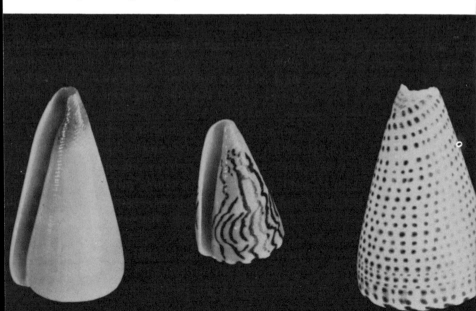

The type and quantity of food often determines the size of the individual and sometimes the ridges on the shell. If food is scarce, shell-building is likely to be suspended until food is more plentiful. If you come upon a big specimen and a small one, it doesn't always mean, though, that one has had better foraging than the other, or is older. It may mean that one is female, the large one, and the other is male. This is especially true where the univalve changes sex and is male early in life and female later.

Some of the univalves, called cones, have an extra organ which we have not found up to this time in any of the mollusks. This is a stinger which can be lethal to man. If one of these live cones is picked up carelessly, it can literally sting to death the man or woman who has done the picking.

The sting is inflicted with a set of syringelike barbed needles which the univalve can protrude from its proboscis. Each needle is connected to a poison sac in the head, and the poison which it contains is extremely potent.

The cones that are known to be able to kill humans are the Marble Cone (*Conus marmoreus*), the Geography Cone (*Conus geographus*), the Courtly Cone (*Conus aulicus*), the Textile Cone (*Conus textile*), and the Tulip Cone (*Conus tulipa*). Some besides these can probably make you very sick; some can cause partial or complete paralysis—some of these might only make you ill if they got less than a perfect chance at you. All these are from the Far Pacific area. The ones in Eastern waters have never proved to be dangerous. But it is the wisest course not to hold your hand over the aperture of any live cone. Also, one you may be holding may not be the cone you think it is. The ones I have mentioned are all very spectacular cones, and just the ones you'd pick up in awe and delight if you hadn't been warned not to. The feeling is said to be that of a bee sting.

These shells do not by any means use this power of theirs exclusively for defense. It is also their weapon for capturing their prey. They stab the prospective meal of fish, crustacean or mollusk, and then wait around till it stops struggling.

They don't have to wait long. Rumphius, the great naturalist, says that partial paralysis in a human begins immediately after a Geography Cone injection. In a shelled mollusk, a creature many times smaller, death would probably be almost instantaneous.

Science Counselor magazine once reported that when an octopus and a venom-producing cone were placed in the same pail and the octopus wrapped a tentacle around the cone, the cone stung the tentacle. The octopus waved the tentacle wildly, later shed it, but died shortly afterward anyhow.

In 1935 on Cayman Island, a man held a cone in his hand and was stung. He was taken to a mainland hospital, according to the medical report, but he was dead upon arrival. The British Museum of Natural History has on display a cone shell whose animal is known to have killed a human. One native of Okinawa knew all about the stinging ability of the particular cone which he picked up to carry to a scientist, yet he was stung in spite of that. He picked up the cone with extreme care but placed it with others in a mesh bag and slung the bag onto his shoulder. The cone stung him in the shoulder from inside the bag. Usually even the poisonous cones will withdraw completely into the shell when threatened. So ordinarily the stinging is a delayed action; usually it does not happen until the cone sticks out its proboscis again.

A vast number of univalves never have anything at all to do with the water. In fact they drown very easily. These are the land and tree snails. The ones that grow in your garden and dine on your best string-bean plants, if you live in northern United States, are likely to be a bit drab. But in Cuba and the Philippine Islands there are some of the brightest-colored snail shells that exist anywhere. In fact Cuba's land snails are the most brilliant anywhere in the world, and the Philippine land snails are only a step behind them. There seem to be a lot of blacks in the Cuban shells; one may be a black shell with red and white lines following the whorls around and around from the apex to the mouth. Another may be a yellow shell with black and white lines following the whorls. There are many thousands of other combinations. Some of the gorgeous color creations have lines of black or red cutting across the whorls; some have many, some have only one or two of these crossing lines. But the effect is tremendous. These are the Polymitas, which grow only in Oriente Province in Cuba. They are like the Coquinas, which we described among the bivalves; the members of one family are shaped the same, but it is well-nigh impossible to find two that are colored alike.

Not only do these snails live away from the sea, but some of them live in the desert. They bury themselves in the ground in the daytime and come out at night. Obviously in this manner they get enough moisture or they wouldn't survive, because all snails must have moisture. But the desert species don't require much. I've already told about the four years a British Museum shell is supposed to have remained alive.

The tree snails, too, are gorgeous. As a rule of thumb, which obviously has many, many exceptions, the land snails are likely to be more round in shape, more flattened toward the apex, while the tree snails are taller and have more pronounced whorls. It has been proved by Dr. R. D. Bales, the well-known private collector, that if tree snails in Florida that grow on one tree are moved to another they will die. They like best the gumbo limbo tree, and a tree called the Jamaica dogwood. But they don't dine on the tree itself; instead they eat plant life that grows on the bark in the form of algae or lichens. If they are shaken off by a high wind, they'll slowly, patiently climb the tree again, and most use the same route. They leave a slime trail where they travel, and it is thought that a snail, finding a trail of this slime, uses it because it provides easier travel over a route that another univalve has reconnoitered. Some tree snails of Cuba (*Liguus poeyanus*) are both right-handed and left-handed in equal numbers, a rarity in the univalve world. Some tropical islands have a lot of tree snails; some others don't have many even though their climate and vegetation seem nearly identical. Yet where two islands, for instance Cuba and the Philippines, have them, the snails are amazingly similar in characteristics even though they are many thousands of miles apart.

Some univalves live in an area which you might describe as being between the habitat of the sea and land mollusks. They live in pools in rocks or on flats. One day their pool will be filled by an exceptionally high tide. The pool may not see any sea water again till the next change of the moon. The next day it may be diluted by a pelting rain until it is, practically speaking, fresh water. The day after may commence a long drought which may leave the snail dependent on dew or left-over moisture under a stone. Even under these conditions, the univalve will grow, seem healthy and reproduce.

All in all, then, the univalves are one-valved mollusks, mostly carnivorous, sometimes herbivorous, and sometimes living as parasites. They produce some of the most beautiful and colorful shells that a collector can find anywhere. They live on land, in the water, and between the two. Their love life is unusual, and they have many ways of getting at and killing other mollusks for food, including poisoning them.

7

How Shells Are Named

I HAVE spoken earlier about the Latin names of the shells, and explained that Latin names are necessary in scientific collections and in trading so that the language barrier can be circumvented. The Latin names mean the same in every country of the world; it is the only language common to world scientists, who are all interested in the findings of other scientists from other countries.

I realize that many, many people don't want to go into shell collecting seriously enough to warrant the learning of Latin names. Even some who have put together quite extensive collections still do not want to bother with Latin. The English names are more graphic, easier to remember, because they are based usually on some appearance characteristic.

But you should know something about how the Latin names are put together so that you won't be totally in the dark if you deal with an expert. Such knowledge is also a base to build on if you want to go on into the upper echelons of shell collecting yourself.

From country to country, common names of shells differ. I have already told you about the Coolie Hat and Keyhole Limpet. There are at least two different Cat's Eyes. The Bubble Shell of China is much different from the Florida Bubble. But the scientific names don't duplicate.

A Swedish naturalist named Karl von Linné set up the

present system of Latin naming flora and fauna in the 1700s. Under it, a shell's first name is the "family" name or the generic name. It tells you the genus to which the shell belongs. The second name is the specific name, and describes for you one shell of that particular species. Sometimes there is a third name, which gives you a variation of one particular shell in that species. This is not, however, often the case. Usually there are only the two Latin words.

And then after the Latin words, either two or three, comes the name of the man who first discovered and is for that reason called the author of the shell. Linné has his name as a part of the names of dozens and dozens of shells. Similarly, other great scientists have their names appearing over and over in the record books as discoverer of some shell. Dall is one of these, Pilsbry is another, Sowerby another. This "authoring" allows a scientist's name to go down in the record books as part reward for the work he has done among the mollusks and in partial recognition of the new facts he has added to the sum of human knowledge.

Sometimes, though, he does not get quite the recognition his work deserves. This happens when his name is long. Then it is usually abbreviated in the shell catalogs and only the scientists, not the casual shell collectors, know for whom the abbreviation stands.

The genus names, of course, appear over and over again. *Busycon, Conus, Cypraea, Fasciolaria, Melongena, Scaphella, Tellina, Tonna* are only a few of them. These are the whelks, the cones, the cowries, the tulips, the conchs, the volutes, the tellins, the tun shells.

These names, then, give you the big "families," the genera. But when the author of the shell gives you the specific names within those main genera, he has the privilege of picking any name he wants. He can name the shell for his wife or somebody else's wife, or anything or anybody whose name can be translated into Latin or Latinized.

In actual practice, however, the author of the shell usu-

28. Long-spined Star Shell (*Astraea longispina* Lamarck)

ally tries in some way to describe the shell. If it is bigger than other members of the family, he may call it *gigantia*. Or if it has the spikes of a crown he will call it *corona*. Other descriptive names that pretty well speak for themselves are *bicolor, corrugata, triangularis, pugilis, contracta, rosea, volcano, pyramidalis, pygmaea* (small or pygmy), *radiata* (with rays). Except for those last two, no translations are needed.

Sometimes that second name, instead of describing a physical characteristic of the shell, describes the place where it was found. *Columbiana, brasilians* (of Brazil), *bermudensis, floridanus, washingtona* are examples of this.

There are a couple of really intricate ones that amuse me because they definitely need no translation in spite of their length if you just split them in two. They are used in connection with *Astraea* (one erroneously), and are *longispina* and *brevispina*. They look imposing, but are of course "long-spined" and "short- or brief (brevity)-spined." So you are again seeing that Latin isn't always as imposing as it seems.

In this same way you can tackle and conquer all the really imposing Latin words. Luckily Latin (unlike English) is a language that is for the most part pronounced just the way it is spelled. No Lord Home that they expect you to pronounce "hume." No Cholmondeley that they expect you to pronounce "chumley." Divide a long and imposing Latin word into syllables, pronounce each syllable, and you have the word.

Sometimes the descriptive second Latin word has nothing whatever to do with the shell itself or where it was found. Then the next most common source would be a person's name. The shell has been named for someone for some reason.

Sometimes the shell is brought to a famous malacologist by an amateur shell collector. If study and research show that this is a new species, then the scientist will author the shell but may decide to name it for the person who discovered it. If it is a man, the word will end in *i*, if it is a woman it will end in *ae*. Thus if somebody wants to name a shell for me, it would be *hoyti*. Or for my wife, *hoytae*.

There was one case of a man who named his new shell after his fiancée, whose name was Maria. She ran off with another (I'm sure, less handsome) man, and the International Commission for Zoological Nomenclature, which rules on such matters, about that time let him know that *mariae* was unacceptable. Perhaps this was because it might sound like a female sea (*maris, mariae*). So he sent in the name *inconstans* for his shell, which served her right.

In line with this, the commission goes with the rule of priority; if several scientists in different parts of the world discover the same shell at about the same time, the first one to discover it and name it is the one whose name stands. Sometimes years later somebody finds that a Latin name in use for a long time was actually predated by an obscure but earlier find. This means that scientists have to give up the old name and get used to the new one. It is, too, a cause for confusion. One book uses the old name, another the newer one, yet it is the same mollusk and shell. For this reason, some of the best-known names have been put on a frozen list which can never be changed; the confusion would be too great. Among these are *Arca, Dentalium, Teredo*. And

I understand that many more well-known names are being considered for this list.

Other changes stem from constantly increasing knowledge on the part of scientists. These changes must be made from time to time. The Horse Conch had its name changed recently from *Fasciolaria gigantea* to *Pleuroploca gigantea*. It did not have the tulip characteristics that it should have had to be classed with the other tulips, so it was changed.

In the matter of that third Latin name, usually it has to do with a subspecies that is the same as the original except that it is smaller or larger, or has some other tiny variation; not different enough to be considered a new shell, but different enough to need noting. *Melongena corona bispinosa* is a perfect example of this. It is a King's Crown Conch exactly like all the rest except that it grows two sets of spines. And *Melongena corona minor* is the same as the regular King's Crown but about half the size. Some scientists won't accept them as subspecies. Some scientists like keeping the genera large and having a lot of subspecies, while others want every tiny difference to have a full name change.

If, then, you find one name for a shell in one book and another in another book, look at the dates on the books and figure that the latest book has the correct new name. This is a fairly accurate rule of thumb.

One very famous shell, *Conus gloria-maris*, is not a three-Latin-word shell. There is a hyphen between the *gloria* and the *maris*, and both words together mean one thing: glory-of-the-seas. A hyphenated word is treated as just one word.

Along with the appropriate names that describe the shell are some fairly puzzling names that don't describe it at all, that are downright misleading. The Mole Cowrie (*Cypraea talpa Linné*) doesn't look like a mole. If you didn't know what a fine scientist Linné was, you'd think he must have been blinder than the mole for which he named the shell. The Zebra Cowrie (*Cypraea zebra Linné*), which looks more like a leopard than a zebra, doesn't increase your confidence in Linné's eyesight. A Tiger Cowrie (*Cypraea tigris Linné*), too, is spotted, not striped; maybe Linné, who was again the culprit, had spots before his eyes.

There are going to be Latin words which you can't figure out if you do much shell collecting. And that stands whether you are a Latin scholar, came within a whisker of flunking your sixth year of it the way I did, or never had any at all. Because this is true, you should provide yourself with a good Latin-English dictionary; that will quickly and painlessly handle any words that you can't figure out at first glance. Armed with this you should have no fears no matter how imposing the name thrown at you.

Latin names, we find, are administered by an international commission. They are three-word names usually, sometime four-word names. The first is the generic name, the second the specific name. If there are four, the third name is a subspecific name, and the last word is always the name of the man who authored or discovered the mollusk. Where there is duplication and confusion of common names between countries, and even in the same country, the scientific names do away with duplication and confusion, and transcend the language barrier among scientists.

8

The History of Shell Collecting

PERHAPS you think that people of our generation, or perhaps the one ahead of ours, were the first ones to collect shells. However the fact is that people have collected shells for thousands of years. In Iraq, near the Euphrates River, archeologists came upon one of their most important finds. They excavated at al 'Ubaid and found, among many other items which gave them a fantastic amount of information about ancient life patterns, seashells and necklaces made of cut pieces of shell. These were underneath many feet of solid clay, which these men proved had been deposited there by flood waters. And some archeologists, because of this, believe that these shells were picked up and that the cut shells were processed *before the Biblical flood.*

If this is true, then the shell collectors who gathered these mollusk skeletons lived an almost unbelievable number of years ago. If these archeologists are wrong, still these shells were collected a respectable number of years back. When the lava-buried city of Pompeii was excavated, shells were found intact under lava.

Other archeologists found cockle shells in the royal tomb of Queen Shub-ad of Ur, in southern Babylonia, who reigned about 2500 B.C.

So as you can see, you're in good company. All this has been going on for a good long while. Nor were these just isolated incidents. The collecting of shells grew and spread instead of languishing.

At first the collecting was fairly utilitarian. The shells were used as utensils. In Queen Shub-ad's tomb, among many other personal items, were cockle shells containing a green cosmetic, perhaps used as eye shadow, perhaps as lip rouge. It may even have been a different color when she died, and the green may have come only with age, though there seems to be no substantiation for this idea.

Shells also were fashioned into weapons and into tools with sharp cutting edges. The less stone that was available in any given area, the more the ancients turned to the use of shells even for axes and knives.

The mollusks that lived in the shells were used as food, especially oysters, which seem to have been as popular in those times as they are today.

Next came the use of shells for personal ornaments. And in order to use them that way, it was necessary somehow to string them so they could be worn. Thus whole shells that lent themselves to stringing were used, and other shells were cut and pierced and thus made into beads. In the caverns of Belgium and France, deep in limestone recesses, shells have been found that had been pierced either for stringing or to be sewed onto clothing, and these date back to the Ice Age.

From the very first, man seems to have been captivated by the beauty of shells, of their lines, their graceful curves, their whorls, their sheen. It was natural, then, that as civilization progressed shells and shell shapes should have had a great influence on the developing art. The shells were copied in gold by the Egyptians. And the Minoans used them extensively in decoration. These seagoing people decorated clay objects with the octopus and its tentacles, or with raised shells.

The gods of these people, especially those that had to do with the sea, were pictured as blowing on shell trumpets, drinking from liquid-filled shells, and the like.

Later the Greeks pictured Aphrodite, who was supposed to have been born of the foam, as rising unclothed from the sea out of an open bivalve. Her Roman counterpart, Venus, was supposed to have emerged the same way, from a huge scallop shell.

When pilgrims visited the Holy Land during pilgrimages and during the Crusades, they were fascinated by the colorful beach scallops. And they brought some of these home when they returned. Thus shells became a symbol of such Holy Land adventures.

Later still the tomb of the Apostle James was supposed to have been discovered through a dream at Santiago de Compostela in northwestern Spain, and when the Holy Land was cut off from pilgrimages by infidels, pilgrims began to go to the tomb of St. James. There they found scallop shells on the nearby beach, and took them home to prove that they had reached their objective. We have a picture of the Apostle James, who was supposed to have preached once in Spain, wearing an inverted scallop shell on the upturned brim of his hat.

This grew into a bit of a racket and three Popes granted the priests of Santiago de Compostela the right to excommunicate anyone who sold scallop shells to pilgrims at any spot except Santiago. Men who made such pilgrimages sometimes returned home and put the scallop shell in their family coat-of-arms. Possession of shells brought from Santiago de Compostela was supposed to keep evil spirits away, and there are many ancient religious paintings which depict Judgment Day, with men rising from graves and holding aloft these scallop shells to protect them from the pitchfork-wielding element waiting on the sidelines for the unrighteous.

It was inevitable that somewhere along the line the shells should take on value. Among the primitive people shells became money. In European countries and in England they were imported for mounting and inlaying and in other ways they became the subject of the jeweler's skill. The Chambered Nautilus shell was a favorite.

In England shells were also used in great quantities by

the rich to cover the walls of rooms, caves, grottoes and above-ground pavilions. The shell pavilion at Goodwood Park, England, was the most ornate; it took seven years to cover the inside with shells in pattern. Some authorities have said that half the great houses in England, at one time during the eighteenth century, had some sort of room inlaid with shells.

Naturally these shells could not be collected in that quantity by the family concerned or by their servants. They would never have come up with the variety necessary even if the task had been possible. So shells were brought in by ships returning from far places, and were bought, sometimes a whole shipload at a time, by the moneyed. This was a great boon to the shipowners since some of the ships would have had to return at least partly in ballast if it had not been for the demand for these bags of exotic shells.

The two matters of increasing shell value and importation were married when enterprising firms began to import shells and then ship them to spots in the world where they were less plentiful and could be used among the natives as we use dollars. The shells were given to the natives in trade for various articles of commerce.

Two enterprising gentlemen began in this way to trade in shells from all parts of the globe. Their names were Marcus Samuel and Samuel Samuel, and the business they started became the Shell Transport and Trading Company. They prospered and in the course of their trading they took on a sideline: petroleum products. Gradually the tail began to wag the dog until today the Shell Company is one of the giant names in oil.

Incidentally, it is an interesting fact, very little-known by the general public, that the Shell Company tankers were each named for a shelled mollusk. And in each case the correct mollusk is on display under glass aboard the ship. Their original ship was the S.S. *Murex.*

Mention of the murex brings up the fantastic story of the influence that tiny mollusks had on the history of the Medi-

29. Murex shells. Top, Three Lace Murex (*Murex florifer Reeve*); center, two Rose Murex (*Murex recurvirostris rubidus R.C. Baker*); bottom, four Apple Murex (*Murex pomum Gmelin*)

30. Endive Murex (*Murex cichoreus Gmelin*)

31. Cowries. Top to bottom: Contracted Cowrie-Helmet (*Cypraecassis coarctata Sowerby*), Carnelian Cowrie (*Cypraea carneola Linné*), Tiger Cowrie (*Cypraea tigris Linné*), Chinese Cowrie (*Cypraea chinensis Gmelin*), Money Cowrie (*Cypraea moneta Linné*)

terranean area, particularly the cities of Sidon and Tyre. These we know today as the Lebanese cities of Saida and Sur.

The murex has a gland on the mantle wall which produces a milklike liquid. This liquid changes in sunlight to yellow, then greenish, then darker to blue, and finally becomes reddish-purple. The Cretans and the Egyptians found out that this fluid would dye cloth permanently. This was somewhere around 1500 B.C.

But Tyre and Sidon took up the art of making this dye so successfully that within 500 years they had a virtual monopoly on the process of extracting it and processing it. The color became known as "Tyrian purple," a term you have heard many times.

Evidently this dying process consisted of crushing the whole animal, or in some cases ripping out the mantle only. These crushed mollusks were tossed into a vat—some authorities say a depression in the rocks—mixed with ingredients which the Tyre and Sidon residents tried hard to keep secret, allowed to stand, and then tested for color.

Modern scientists have attempted to make dye of murex shells and have found that it takes some 10,000 mollusks to make around a twentieth of an ounce of the liquid. So you can see how fantastically expensive the stuff must have been. And how depleted the murex animals in any area that manufactured much of the dye must have become.

There was one direct result of this: exploration. The demand for the dye was there. Religious draperies and clothes were dyed with it. Even a full set of sails for Cleopatra's royal barge was thus dyed. Clothing was made from Tyrian purple for the very few who could afford it. It became what we'd call today a status symbol.

When the supplies of murex mollusks began to give out, explorers went on expeditions in search of more. Huge piles of murex shells have been found in many Mediterranean areas such as Sicily, Malta and Cadiz, places which did not themselves produce the dye. It is assumed by historians that these areas were colonized primarily as the result of murex searching. They acted as stations for collecting the mollusks and possibly even engaged in some sort of preliminary processing to cut down on the weight and bulk of what was sent back to Tyre and Sidon.

As the result of the dye, Tyre and Sidon became trading and money centers and grew extremely rich. Tyrian coins even had a murex shell imprinted on them.

This dye color was mentioned in the Bible, and referred to by writers of ancient times, Pliny and Plutarch and others. The industry grew and grew. "Born to the purple" today has come to signify born to riches and authority. Certainly it took plenty of money to wear it in those times.

But then in Rome, laws were passed which finally sounded the death knell for this great industry. First the purple was restricted to Senators and the trappings of the Church. And then Emperor Nero decreed that only the emperor himself could wear the purple. It had grown to be such a status symbol that the ruler wished to be the only one privileged to use it. And this was, of course, the beginning of the end. You can't carry forward an industry, the chief source of wealth for two great cities, on the clothing needs of one man —no matter how wealthy he may be. Probably the industry catered for a while to areas which did not feel the full weight of Rome's power. But gradually it died. What an astonishing story, though; the rise and fall of so great an industry and two such great cities, all based on a small univalve.

The trade in shells grew. The Money Cowrie became the bread-and-butter shell. It was used like our silver coins. At one time in West Africa, a young healthy wife could be purchased for 60,000 cowrie shells, not necessarily Money Cowrie, and a run-of-the-mill wife for 20,000. A pipe and one pipeload of tobacco, though, only cost 12 shells—which probably only goes to prove that in those days and among those primitive people, just as today, a young man would pay a great deal more for female companionship, even poor female companionship, than he would for an evening spent at home with a good pipe.

This Money Cowrie mollusk came mostly from very warm areas such as the Indian Ocean and the equatorial islands of the Pacific. In spite of that fact it has been discovered in archaeological diggings almost everywhere, even in Russia and the Scandinavian peninsula and beside our own Tennessee River. Thousands of tons of these shells were collected, carried on backs, on pack animals, and by water, and used for barter and trade.

Among some African tribes, and some other primitive peoples, the cowrie shell, partly because of its shape, became the symbol of fecundity. It was given as a gift to the bride, or sewn onto her clothing, if any, or hung around her neck.

In our own country, the Money Cowries dug up in Alabama are thought to have been brought over to this country for Indian barter aboard one of Columbus' ships, or some other that sailed here soon after that. The United States National Museum thinks that only the first ships would have brought these; when word got back home that our eastern Indians were not particularly interested in them, no more would have been sent. Other Money Cowries dug up in northcentral United States and in Canada are thought to have been brought to this continent by the Hudson's Bay Company and traded by them to the Cree and Montagnais Indians for furs.

Shells dug up in this way have been a great help in determining trade routes used by Indians on our continent and by primitive peoples on the European and African continents. Shells from the Red Sea have been found in England in graves dug long before the shell-importation era in that country. Geographers have thus found shells invaluable in their work of mapping the wanderings of prehistoric man; geologists use the fossil forms of shells to date geological formations. Shell fossils go back past the Paleozoic era. And of course malacologists and conchologists spend their scientific lives in the study of these shells and the creatures that form them.

In the United States, in the same way, evidences of trade between the Indian tribes has been established and the routes plotted out by the presence of seashells dug up in the burial places of inland tribes that should have had no seashells, tribes that had never been near the sea. These tribes are thought to have made trade contact at certain points with seashore tribes. One inland tribe, for instance, had beautiful wampum, but no one could find piles of debris from its manufacture. It wasn't until the twentieth century that huge piles of such debris were found clear down on the coast of the Gulf of California. The Indians, being nobody's fools, had manufactured the wampum where the shells were, and simplified a transportation problem immeasurably.

Wampum was of two major kinds: whole tusk shells in strings, popular in the Northwest Pacific area, and cut pieces of clam shell strung together, common among the eastern tribes. In the 1600s, even after European settlers came to these shores, most of the trading was done with wampum. Only gradually did this custom die out.

The eastern wampum was of two kinds, purple and white. The purple was cut from what we now call Quahog shells, and only the colored portion was used. The white was made from the center stalk of whelk shells and was only about half as valuable as the purple. White was also made from the part of the Quahog shell that wasn't used for making purple wampum.

Wampum had several names at first: roanoke, peak, peag, and others. But later it was all lumped together by the white settlers as wampum. It was measured in cubits, which was the distance from the elbow to the tip of the little finger. A big man with long arms couldn't afford to sell wampum, but he could make a great bargain in buying it. The short

32. Atlantic Deer Cowrie (*Cypraea cervus Linné*)

man had exactly the opposite problem. The chances are if
the big Indian intended to give wampum in trade he sent
a short friend to do the bargaining and paying.

Making the wampum was never easy. Certain kinds, used
locally in our Middle Atlantic coast, were made of whole
shells and so were fairly easy to make. But because of this
they wouldn't buy much. The strings of high-priced wampum had to be cut and polished and pierced, all of which
was very hard work. An Indian who made wampum had to
put the full value of the finished product into it, in his own
expended time. The value of wampum thus corresponded
to the time it took to make it. The Indian who used it paid
that symbol of expended time for the product he received.
Or if he received it (for furs perhaps) he received that symbol of someone else's time in return for the time he had
used in catching the animal and preparing the pelt.

When the European settlers came, blacksmiths tried to
make wampum and gave it up as a bad job. At first they

could find no shortcut, and they had to put almost twice as much time into the making as they should have, to have been paid its value. Later on, though, with better tools, Dutch settlers managed to make a lot of wampum, so much that wampum became worthless for trading purposes.

While it was still in use, though, it had several advantages. The Indian could wear it and in doing so ornament himself. At the same time he was guarding his worldly possessions. He had money at hand, too, when he needed it.

Because of the flooding of the supply wampum was not legal tender much after the mid-1600s. Still, it was used here and there for some time after that. One of the ferry boats in New York harbor accepted it clear to the turn of the seventeenth century in return for a ride.

Whereas the white settlers' counterfeiting of the Indian wampum caused the discontinuance of its use, there is at least one instance in shell history where counterfeiting took an amazing turn.

In early years the Precious Wentletrap was so high-priced in the Orient, and so scarce, that some very clever Chinese artisans made almost perfect replicas out of rice-flour paste. They were so good that they fooled people for many years until a collector, cleaning a shell one day, watched it melt away.

Much later a number of beds of these shells were found, and the value went down correspondingly as the supply rose. Instead of being worth several hundreds of dollars, their value dropped to around a dollar.

But, the amazing part of the story is that the counterfeits had been so wonderful that as they grew scarce and the fame of their perfection was spread abroad, more people wanted to own them. They kept increasing in value until they are now far, far more valuable than the real shells, and some have been traded for more than the earlier value of the real shells.

The tusk-shell wampum used on our West Coast was as hard to produce as the eastern wampum. We have spoken in the chapter on mollusks about the shape of the tusk shells. Since these already had lengthwise holes and needed only stringing, it would seem as if they should have been easy to prepare. The preparation was easy, all right. But getting the shells wasn't. The Indians did it with primitive long-handled rakelike instruments with which they raked into the bottom sand and mud from a canoe in an effort to bring up these shells. Then the animal had to be removed.

Wampum made from whole tusk shells was very valuable. Wampum made from short or broken pieces was twenty times less valuable. Again the value was measured by the length. In California, cut pieces of abalone shell were used for money and were immensely valuable compared to ordinary wampum. Their greater value may have stemmed from the fact that the braves considered that they looked very well wearing these strings. They were never willing to part with anything that ornamental, except grudgingly and in return for a great deal of value.

In the meantime scientists in Europe had begun to study mollusks, to compare, to classify and to name. We have mentioned Linné as being the father of the present Latin naming system.

One of the first collectors in England seems to have been John Tradescant. He traveled a lot on various missions and collected everything in Nature that he could carry home. A big part of his collection was shells; the whole thing passed to his son John, Jr., who founded a museum with it. Elias Ashmole helped him with the museum, finally gained control of it, and it became the Ashmolean Museum at Oxford.

In the same way Sir Hans Sloane collected shells all over the world, bought others to the tune of about £60,000, and willed his collections to Britain. It became the nucleus of the British Museum of Natural History.

Men were by then treating shells not as ornaments or as money, but as animals to be studied by naturalists.

A contemporary of the men mentioned, Martin Lister, produced the first really ambitious book on shells, the *His-*

toria Conchyliorum, with almost 1,000 engravings of shells.

The Dutch, too, had a wonderful opportunity to collect shells through the Dutch East India Company and its trade throughout the world. It was probably during this period that rare shells began to take on value dependent on their scarcity.

The Duchess of Portland assembled what was at that period the largest collection in Europe. Linné came and admired it; some of Cook's shells, collected on his trips around the world, made their way into it. She, however, appears to have been not so much a naturalist as a collector with plenty of money.

From these beginnings, shell collecting has grown parallel to the growth and speed of transportation. The pilgrims on foot or on horseback collected. Sailing vessels brought back new and exotic shells from far places. Rail transportation brought our two coasts closer together, in time and ease of travel, and this had its effect on the transporting of the shells of one coast to the other.

Now the plane has brought the great shell-gathering areas within hours of each other. If a collector had the money and a two-weeks' vacation, he could shell Sanibel Island, Japan, the Philippines, and the Great Barrier Reef, all on regularly scheduled flights. He might be a bit short on sleep and ready for another vacation when he finished, but he could do it.

The United States, though it never had the colonies that Holland and England had, and though it is a much younger country, can boast fantastic collections in its museums. The United States National Museum in our capital has just under 10,000,000 shell items; the Smithsonian Institute collection is fabulous, as is that of the Philadelphia Museum of Natural History. As a result of ease of travel, you find shells of far places where you least expect them. There's a valve of a Giant Clam in front of a restaurant a few miles from my home in Vermont. In my town there is a very fine cowrie collection owned by a young man whose company first sent him to Hawaii. If my town has these things, other towns must have similar shell curiosities to boast about.

Besides the pedestrian methods of shell distribution, there have been a number not so pedestrian. In early days, as I mentioned before, ships often returned from trading in far places at least partly in ballast. And that ballast was sometimes bags of seashells. When shells no longer had value in trade they were sometimes treated like other ballast and heaved overboard before entering home port. Ballast Point, outside San Diego, was said to have been named for this custom. Where rock or sand ballast usually stayed where it landed, shells often came ashore. At one time shells from far places could be found regularly on Ballast Point.

In the same way Pacific shells have been picked up on Cape Cod, possibly from a wrecked ship, and far-away shells appeared on Long Island Sound beaches during World War II when ships returned from England in ballast after carrying war supplies.

Among other famous cases known to most shell collectors was the incident of the ship with the cargo of abalone shells for use as inlay in the furniture trade. It was sunk near the coast of Cuba, and for years afterward these very lovely shells were washed up on Cuban beaches, much to the astonishment and delight of the residents of that area.

Another incident which has become famous is that of a sailing ship which was wrecked off Cumberland Head while returning to England with a cargo of cowrie shells. Here again for years afterward the shells washed ashore, and this confused laymen and even scientists because they continued to come in for such a long time. At first these people were sure cowries couldn't exist in water that cold. But when they kept washing up, it shook some of the less knowledgeable.

On Sanibel Island a practical joker imported a box of cheap, showy shells from Japan, scattered them on the beach in front of his cottage, and moved his chair out where he could hear the awed excitement of the shellers who picked them up. Undoubtedly, like the English incident, this caused a bit of scientific misdirection.

In the same area, a cottage on Fort Myers Beach, Florida, which contained a lovely collection of shells from everywhere, was washed away in a hurricane and broken up. Shells from Japan, from even the Great Barrier Reef of Australia, appeared on neighboring beaches for years. Incidents like this have made the collection of shells from far-off places very easy indeed for those skillful or lucky enough to benefit.

In World War II our armed forces were stationed on Pacific islands and on mainland beaches. Our occupation forces were later in Japan. Some of our technical experts were also sent to Australia and New Zealand. These men on occasion had time to themselves, sometimes a lot of time either while waiting for action or during furlough. Many, many of these men must have picked up the shells of their particular region and brought them home for their families to see and admire.

I have first-hand information about the extent of all this. In May 1965, the *Reader's Digest* published an article of mine about shell collecting. I got literally hundreds of letters in response to it. And with one or two exceptions these people wanted information about shells which they or some member of their families had brought home from the Pacific in World War II. Fully half of those letters wanted to know how the writer could sell the shells. One woman said she had several Glory-of-the-Seas Cones, and I wrote her that I doubted it, but that if she really did, life had been very good to her financially. Some of them admitted tacitly to needing money at the moment. A few said it outright.

If that many people wrote me (most people either would not write or would write or contact some shell collector, dealer, or museum they knew about), think of the tremendous number of people who must own World War II Pacific shells.

The same article was postponed in the foreign edition of

the magazine until the August issue. So I had just about finished with the first batch of letters when another batch began to arrive from Taiwan, the Philippines, and such far places. This time people wanted to know about a list of American traders or dealers. It cost them about thirty cents to write and cost me thirty cents, each, to reply—which touched my ego in one way and my pocketbook in a very different way. It also astonished me in what it seemed to prove.

Shells have been an increasing influence in the world in still other areas. Their shapes have been used by architects in planning building arches, building ornaments, spiral staircases, and in other phases of their work.

From those first jeweled mountings for the Chambered Nautilus, the mounting of shells, the copying of them in precious metals, has gone on.

Buttons are made from cheap shells, and many kinds of shells are ingeniously turned into all sorts of shapes and figures to become part of a $6,000,000-a-year shell industry which even has an outlet, of all places, clear up in Vermont. Besides the regular shells themselves, which are sold in these shops, there are figurines, all kinds of shell flowers, handbags trimmed with shells, desk accessories decorated with shells, shells for vases and lamps.

Shells have been part of religious ceremonies throughout the ages. In Japan the Shinto sect calls its members to worship by blowing on a Triton's Conch. The Japanese Triton's Conch is a much more beautifully colored shell than our own. A shell is used in Italy to "shivaree" newlyweds. India and Tibet have both used shells as trumpets; whether or not Tibet still does is not known because of the Communist takeover. In Puerto Vallarta, on a deep bay of Mexico's west coast, when Mrs. Hoyt and I were there, peddlers blew on a shell to announce their passage down the street so that housewives would come out and buy. The shell I saw was blown through a mouthpiece glued or cemented into a hole bored in one of the whorls. But most are blown through a hole made by cutting off the tip of the apex. Other places in Mexico use shells as trumpets in other ways. We were told that some were used as speaking trumpets to give medicine men an eerie voice. It was always good for business when such men could make chills travel the spines of their patients, if that is what you would call those who consult a medicine man.

Polynesian babies are bathed in a tub made of half a Giant Clam. These shells are also used as fonts for holy water in the temples of some European Catholic churches even today. In India the Indian Chank Shell is considered to be sacred. It is a univalve seldom more than half a foot in length. Right-handed Indian Chank Shells are used by the people as trumpets at points in the ceremony. But the left-handed Indian Chank Shell is extremely rare, and most of these are mounted in gold and are held during the ceremony. The priest holds the shell in his hand, and at one point recites a chant to it telling it that it is adored, telling it why they worship it, and asking that they be filled with joy.

We have spoken about the inky material from the octopus and squid. This was the base of India ink (very black indelible ink) until the chemical industry found a cheaper and easier substitute.

The byssus of the pen shell has threads that are very soft. These were collected in olden times and woven into various articles of apparel, notably gloves. Since there are comparatively few threads to the pen animal, the collecting of them and making them into yarn was a very time-consuming chore. So these gloves became a status symbol, although to a lesser degree than the wearing of the purple. In 1754 a pair of stockings was said to have been made of these threads for Pope Benedict XIV, so sheer that a jeweled snuffbox contained them.

There is a large jingle shell in the area of the Philippines

33. Jingles (*Anomia simplex Orbigny*)

and China known as the Window Shell. The isinglass-like material that these are made of is in layers and can be split into sheets, which in turn can be cut into squares. They are set in frames when used as windows. This material still takes the place of glass there because, disregarding the cost element and the nonavailability of glass in primitive areas, the shell material is wind-resistant in a land where there are sometimes heavy typhoons. And it cuts down the amount of light, which in tropical areas is an advantage.

So we find that from earliest recorded time, hundreds of years before Christ came to this earth, shells have been gathered and hoarded for their usefulness, for their beauty. They have been used as money, as inspiration for architecture, and as an invaluable help to archeologists. Museums acquired huge collections; men have made a life work of studying them and the mollusks that make them. And each year more collectors are added to the present army who collect them either intermittently or seriously. Each year, too, they are distributed more and more widely, many of them halfway around the world from the place they were grown. A history of shell collecting would read like the history of the world.

9

Beach Collecting

BEACH collecting is the backbone of the shell-collecting hobby. Far more shells are picked up dead from some beach than by wading, diving, dredging and trading all combined. The beachgoer of once or twice a year may not collect often, and what he takes may be by sophisticated standards "trash," but he takes an awful lot. And there are a tremendous number of these casual collectors who come up with literally tons and tons of shells every year.

In beach collectors you run the gamut from the man who has read about that particular shell beach and feels he must "see" it the way he sees Disneyland or Knott's Berry Farm or Silver Springs, to the unobtrusive walker who bends over only a few times in several careful miles, so well does he know his shells.

The first usually accosts you on the beach and says, "Where are all the valuable shells? The *big* shells?" His tone implies that it's your fault that big $100 specimens aren't lying out in sight everywhere. The other man is happy if he finds one tiny specimen that is new to him or better than something he already has. You have all the gradations in between.

The so-this-is-a-shell-beach-where-are-all-the-shells family we'll examine, but not at great length. Instruction would be wasted on them until they've worked that pick-up-everything-big complex out of their systems.

Usually you can tell them by their clothes. They're dressed

34. A typical "shelling beach." Note the many old pen shells.

for sightseeing; they probably have several other "points of interest" they intend to "see" that day, and those require dressing.

But the shells and the beach do their work; it's a subtle web of magic they weave, but it's pretty persuasive. And the first thing you know, these people, who have been so scornful on arrival, see something in calcium that is colorful or shapely or both, and one of them picks it up. He shows it to the rest of the party, and one of *them* has meantime found something that *he* considers twice as colorful or shapely or interesting. So he shows that. A third spots a *very* interesting shell, only it is out in the edge of the wash. So he sits down and whips off his shoes and his socks and rolls up his trouser legs and goes after it. This is an inspiration. The women take off their stockings and shoes, and one of them, wearing pince-nez on a gold chain and looking as if she should be introducing the speaker for the Fortnightly Club, holds up the front of her dress to make a basket for their finds until Joe can go back to the car and get the empty lunch basket and two or three plastic bags they had planned to use for vegetables.

So they progress up the beach, shedding coats, shoes, neckties, shirts and the like in piles as they go, becoming more relaxed about their appearance all the time. And picking up the most horrible assortment of big pen shells, broken whelks, ark shells, Horse Conchs that look like something in wool that the moths had been after. They pick up columellas, olives with the points gone, chunks of shell that are colorful or worn smooth by the waves, chunks of shell that you can't imagine why they pick up. They pick up horseshoe crabs, sea urchins, starfish, whelk egg cases. Anything big they pick up. They mostly forget all about the other places they had intended to see. "We can go there the next cold day." As the sun sinks low they start back for the car regretfully, stopping to add an occasional irresistible item as they progress. They look like pack animals whose master was heading for the gold rush. The picnic basket is piled high, a broken pen shell that shows iridescent purple on top of everything and a couple of those egg cases hanging down over the side. The plastic bags, full, are slung over shoulders, and one of the party is gathering up and carrying all the discarded clothing as she comes to it.

This is objective reporting, not sneering, on my part. Because everybody has to start this way. Maybe everybody won't start with big and broken items, but everybody will collect specimens that will curl the lips of other collectors further along. And that holds clear into the upper echelons.

A fine collector said to me recently, "My daughter is bringing in the darndest things, common and broken. But I say nothing and clean them for her, because she's having a wonderful time."

That's the whole thing right there. She, and these by-the-day people we've just been talking about, have had a wonderful time. Pretty soon she, or they, will come back again because they had such fun. And having had these big items now, they'll find themselves a shade more discriminating that next time. And the time after that, still a shade further in that direction.

Perhaps meanwhile they will have talked to people, read this book or some other that will hasten the discrimination process. They'll begin to look for certain things. And right there a new shell collector is launched on his or her hobby career. It may go far or it may not. As it progresses, knowledge will be garnered; as knowledge is garnered, the hobby will progress still further.

We'll assume the person is hooked, is excited by shell collecting and its challenges. He or she may start coming to the beach every day. The next vacation, perhaps he'll rent a cottage right on a beach that has shells.

After a few years, perhaps he may buy a home or a cottage on a shell beach. This takes us to the person who spends time (possibly a whole lot of it) on a shell beach, poking, looking, walking, picking up. These people are the cream. They're the distillate, the dedicated. And daily contact with others dedicated makes for even deeper dedication. As I've said, I like and admire these people very much indeed. Perhaps if I tell you about them, individually and collectively, you will feel you might like them too, might enjoy knowing them, might even like to try for a while being one of them.

When they're living next to a shell beach, be it for a short or long period, these people live and breathe shells. On the beach that I frequent, your friends don't greet you as they meet you shelling with "Good morning." They say, "Any Junonias today?" At the hotels and restaurants at mealtime the news spreads like a wave from table to table that "Mrs. So-and-So found a Golden Olive, my dear. And it was"—here the voice takes on hushed reverence—"*live!* The point was perfect. I saw it myself. A lovely shell. And they say Mrs. Whumpsis had walked past that spot not three minutes before. She's literally livid."

The same information is passed from person to person as they meet on the beach. If a couple of nonshelling or back-resting husbands go to the fishing pier, they hear it there. And of course the shell shops are a clearing house for such items. The more they can whip up interest, the better for business. Mrs. Whumpsis in her disappointment may *buy* a Golden Olive the day she starts for home.

These people have one thing in common with the once-

35. Junonias (*Scaphella junonia* Shaw) were named for the voluptuous goddess, Juno.

a-year sheller: they worry less and less about their appearance while shelling. They come upon one combination of clothing for warm weather and another for cold weather that are comfortable for them. These are called shelling Outfits. Like scallops and Coquinas, no two shelling Outfits are exactly alike.

Warm-weather Outfits are likely to be pretty amazing. But they are nothing when compared to cold, north-storm Outfits. Warm-weather wear goes in heavily for bathing suits, sun bonnets, wide-brimmed straws, and scarfs of incredible design tied under the chin. These all result from an effort to beat the heat, the blistering sun, and the mosquitoes, and the whole apparition usually smells of either suntan lotion or citronella.

The most interesting warm-weather Outfit I ever saw was on a lovely young lady. She was wearing a flesh-colored bikini but was completely encased in transparent mosquito netting, a combination that produced a rather startling effect. She carried a huge pocketbook into which she was squirreling her finds.

I saw the next most amazing Outfit after a hurricane that brought beautiful shells up onto Sanibel Island Beach together with pools of water that bred clouds of small black, nonhumming mosquitos. Two elderly female shellers appeared in harem pants, wide-brimmed straw hats, and mosquito netting draped over the hats. They had cut two armholes in the mosquito netting for convenience. Shelling was fabulous and they soon ran out of room for their finds in baskets, so they began to cache them in the legs of their tight-at-the-ankles harem pants. By the time they were quite bulky down below and clicked when they walked, they were an arresting sight.

But the cold-weather Outfits take the cake. Here shellers seem to let themselves go. Once during a cold spell I saw a sheller wearing a good-will-bag-type overcoat with abrasions, which had been black but had yellowed with salt spray. A derby hat, held on with a scarf tied under the chin, swimming trunks, and a pair of rubber galoshes, one of which the dog had been chewing, completed this ensemble. Note the absence of trousers.

I felt sorry that this man's finances forced him to wear these clothes until I saw him being driven to Bailey's General Store in a long limousine by a uniformed chauffeur.

One of the best-known jurists in the country wears white beach shoes, bathing trunks, and an old-fashioned bathrobe. The bottom of the bathrobe he gathers and pulls up under the tassled cord around his waist, way up out of the way. The effect is of half a bulky bathrobe moving on two bare legs. He hangs a flat basket on his arm and arranges the specimens he selects very neatly inside.

At warm-area winter resorts, wherever they are, when there's a north storm and a cold wave, the people huddle indoors around the fire and curse the weather. Not so on a shell beach; here the people put on their Outfits and go happily forth to shell. They know that they'll have good weather and bad shelling, or bad weather and good shelling. And they much prefer the good shelling.

Hooded parkas are common on good shell beaches in cold weather, the drawstring fastened under the chin, the hood coming to a point above the head. This, usually without pants but with the inevitable galoshes (the beach is likely to be wet where the shells are), completes that Outfit. You speak to the two eyes, the nose and the mouth that show, saying, "Good morning, sir." A woman's voice is likely to answer.

The methods of collecting are as varied as the Outfits. You can adopt or discard any of these ideas I'm going to give you for your own shelling. To begin with, a great many shellers carry some sort of stick to help them poke into piles of shells. These can be just plain sticks, or they can be canes, which for older shellers serve a dual purpose. Or they can be, and often are, light aluminum implements with a hand-with-fingers end on them, made by some enterprising firm precisely for shell collecting. You can rake over the piles with the fingers, slide a desirable shell into the hand part and pick it up.

Between the simple stick and the aluminum implement there is everything. I've seen a little kid's toy garden rake lashed onto the end of a broomstick. I've seen a stick with a rake lashed to one end and a tin cup nailed to the other end for picking up the shells.

I thought I'd seen the ultimate when I looked out one day and saw a man poking over the piles of shells with a golf club. I spoke of this to my landlord and he explained that the man was Gene Sarazen. After I found that out, the thing made sense.

There is one woman whom I talked with who has a special pair of bifocal glasses made only for shelling. The oculist furnishes her the optimum prescription for the exact distance between her eyes and her feet, not between her eyes and a printed page held in her lap.

There are competitors among shellers. Many nights I've looked out the window and seen a flashlight beam moving slowly along the beach, searching. Someone is afraid that someone else will beat him to a rare shell and he is making a careful examination of the tide line just before he drops into bed early. Why does he drop into bed early? So he can be operating again before daylight. And I have risen in the morning while it was still dark and seen a flashlight beam searching the tide line again.

It somehow grows very important, as others show their finds and accept plaudits, to find a wonderful shell yourself and accept equal time from one and all. Applause is heady stuff. And make no mistake, if you go into it head over heels you gradually get the feeling that winning the Nobel Prize is fine, but not in the class with finding a Junonia. Leave the beach for home and by the end of the first day you're back to normal and wonder how you could have felt that way. But while you're there and under the influence of the ardent shellers around you, that's how it is.

Most people react reasonably and, if they find nothing spectacular, take their disappointment in stride and determine to see if during their next visit their luck will change. But now and then one resorts to lying. A minister, of all people, staying at one of our inns, showed two small matching Junonias and said he had found them close together on the beach that morning. He was in the midst of basking in the admiration and envy of one and all in that dining room when a woman arrived and announced that she had just been talking to the shell dealer who had sold the minister two matching small Junonias a few hours before. The result was acute embarrassment for all concerned.

Most regular shellers are friendly. They speak to each other and show each other shells whether they've met formally or not. You may talk with a man for years on the beach and consider him a friend and never know anything but his first name in all that time. But don't speak to the very white, dressed-up day-sheller unless he speaks first; you're likely to be stared through coldly if you do.

Now and then there are exceptions. Once, every day for two weeks my wife Marg and I encountered one of the very few unfriendly people among the regular shellers. Each time we spoke; each time she elevated her nose and didn't. But one day when we were about to pass her she planted herself squarely in front of us. Beaming, she said, "A very interesting beach today. I *found* my Junonia."

Because Junonias are so highly prized on Florida beaches, there are all sorts of tales about them. There was the battle ax who spotted one at the same time a man approaching from the other direction saw it and reached for it. Completely in character, she stood on his outstretched fingers while she triumphantly acquired it for herself.

As I've intimated, there are shellers who, delightful people away from the beach, on the matter of shelling are a bit hard to take. The pseudo-experts are among them. Not the real experts; it's not necessary for them to impress anybody. But in the case of the unsure expert it is.

For instance, even if you pick up what you consider to be a perfect specimen of a rare shell, a pseudo-expert is likely to eye it blankly. A good poker player looks animated compared with a pseudo shell expert examining somebody else's rare shell. He'll raise his eyebrows if it's a bivalve and say, "Not double?" And if it's a univalve he'll say, "What, no operculum?"

There was one pseudo-expert who made a fetish of Latin names. A doctor handled *her* nicely by suddenly asking her, "Have you seen my hemophilia?" They say she spent days trying to find it in the shell book.

I have heard that some hotel owners aren't above planting a few medium-fine shells on their beaches in the early morning to keep up the interest and increase the length of some stays. But I have never caught any of them at it and I doubt it. However, I do know of one incident of beach salting which had the blessing of one and all.

Some years back a school for the crippled in Miami made arrangements to bring a busload of students to see Sanibel Island's shell beach. Would there be any possibility that on crutches or in their wheelchairs, they could do a little shelling?

Not only would this be possible, the local shell club heard about it, got together and asked for donations of duplicates. They wanted, too, fine shells that weren't quite as perfect as the best the collector had, but were far better than most people can ever find. The response was heartwarming.

On the day of the children's arrival a hard-packed section of beach in a remote area was chosen and salted with those donated shells until it was like no beach ever has been before or since. They say there were even a few shells from far-off places under the theory that they were fine shells and none of the children would know the difference or care if they did.

After the beach was finished and ready, the local Boy Scouts stood guard over it to make sure that a by-the-day tourist didn't strike a bonanza.

The crippled kids came, moved up and down the beach in the chairs and on the crutches, shrieking with delight. They found, one after another, the lovely shells made ready for them. And the fact that some of them were oiled and polished probably meant nothing to them.

They had a marvelous, exciting time, and for some of them that kind of time must have been hard come by. Their eyes were shining and bright as they compared finds and called to each other. Finally they were loaded back into the bus. The amazing part is that the people connected with the effort probably felt as good and enjoyed the experience every bit as much as the kids did.

There are hints about beach shelling which might help you find unusual shells that others might miss. First off, get a tide table and watch the tides. Plan your shelling around that. A minus, or extra low, tide, which comes in winter with the change of the moon, is a day for which you should make extensive plans. The water will go clear out, and sections of beach that are usually under water will be high and dry; bars that are usually covered will be exposed. Also pools behind these bars will be quiet and will often clear up to the point where you can see everything on the bottom.

When a minus tide comes along, you should be out on the exposed bars barefoot or should be wading those pools.

When there is a storm, the waves will sweep high on the beach. And you should patrol that high-water line because shells are being washed in with every wave. Others will be doing the same thing, and the person who first reaches the spot where a fine shell is being rolled out into sight will be the winner. Storms produce fantastic numbers of shells to reward the knowledgeable sheller. It's during storms that you are likely to get live specimens on the beach where normally there are only dead shells.

If you are shelling at mean tide, examine the tide line as you shell in one direction. But when you return, examine the high-tide line. People always tend to shell next to the water, and sometimes the high-tide line of a few hours before is neglected. If you come out at mean tide and find the beach being patrolled at the water's edge by numbers so great that your chances of getting anything you want are cut way down, then start right in with the high-tide line. You may be very nicely rewarded. Marg's Junonia came in this way; she was on a return walk home, moving very fast but watching the upper part of the beach, when she came upon it lying there. Obviously from the position of the tide line, that Junonia must have been lying there in plain sight for several hours.

When competition on the beach is at its worst, get into your car and drive to some other area of beach less crowded. If you can't do that, you have one other chance. You may still score heavily by slowing down far, far slower than even your normal careful pace. Study each inch of beach carefully. Turn over all clumps of seaweed washed up and examine what is clinging to them. When you come to shell piles, sit down and go over the whole pile, maybe spending an hour right in that one place. By moving the top layer of shells that all the others have seen, you are examining shells that may have been hidden from them.

Turning over seaweed is a good bet whether there's competition or not. And you should take nothing for granted. Turn over pen shells. If they're open, look inside. Recently a woman showed me a live shell in excellent condition, whose animal had been so intent on feasting on a pen that it had not abandoned its dinner as the pen was rolled ashore. By the time the woman came along they were both high and dry.

Some shells, such as the Boat Shell and the Jewel Box, are usually found attached to some other shell such as a pen shell. Keep an eye out for these two and others like them when you're turning things over.

There are people on any beach worthy of being called a shell beach who will claim that by carefully checking the angle of a storm wind, they can go directly to the section where the best shells will be rolling in on that particular day.

I never doubt these people out loud. I only know that I am personally unable to perform this feat, and I have never been with anybody who could on the particular day I was with him. He always seems to have done it yesterday or in last week's storm, but he never does it while I am with him.

However, if you yourself consistently find some particular shell in quantity in one place when some particular wind is blowing, return to that spot if you want specimens of that shell.

Under no circumstances make the mistake of thinking that because one shell is plentiful on your beach when you arrive there, it is going to be plentiful tomorrow or next week or next month or next year. These things run in cycles when a bed of shells is, in some way, disturbed somewhere and many of its shells are washed in.

Once the semi-rare Lion's Paw (*Lyropecten nodosus*

Linné) washed in live on Sanibel Island's beaches in such quantities that one of the inns decided to serve Lion's Paw chowder. In most places an inn's guests would have had no idea they were seeing molluscan history made. But the guests there knew, and they ordered the chowder almost unanimously to be able to say they had been in on this only-time-ever event. All the shells were reverently processed and some of them are still around.

They say, too, that one day at one spot on Captiva Island you could pick up Golden Olives about as fast as you could reach over. A man I know gathered all he could find, processed them, and for years afterward had the very finest trading bait that anyone could ask for. By sending them to far places he received lovely shells in return.

So if you find a bonanza in specimens of some particular shell that is normally hard to find or semi-hard, take advantage of the situation. It is always easier to discard unwanted shells than it is to find them when they aren't there. A couple of years ago pectens came in live in amazing numbers. I've kicked myself ever since because I didn't gather up hundreds of these live scallops in hundreds of different color patterns. But I took a few of the most colorful and was going to get others in other years. The result? You guessed it: they haven't been back like that since.

Actually there's no substitute for knowing the shells cold when it comes to success in beach shelling. And this comes only from practice, from seeing them over and over, parts, chunks, whole shells, and identifying them. As you train yourself, your shelling eye grows sharper and sharper until it knows and automatically catalogs everything it falls on. Once Marg and I were walking the middle beach, fast, because so many were next to the water at that spot. And suddenly, between two shellers, a large, rounded, scalloptype shell raised and lowered a valve. Only that.

The two people within three feet of it saw this but didn't interpret it. We knew that it must be a live Fan with the rounded side up. We waited till they had moved on. We

36. Lion's Paws *(Lyropecten nodosus Linné)*, so named because of its bulbous "knuckles."

went over and picked it up, the first live Zigzag Scallop Fan *(Pecten ziczac Linné)* either of us had ever found. You should practice identifying shells every chance you get.

When you first start beach collecting you may be fooled by the color of your shell specimen. When you take it out of the collecting container at home, the shell you had been so proud of may look frightful. You wonder what could have been the matter with your eyesight.

It's not your eyesight. It's just that wet shells look colorful; after they dry out, some will seem drab and chalky. Sometimes oil will help this, but it is best to develop an eye for telling and discarding these before you go to the trouble of lugging them around. If the shell looks worn or has little pin-point holes when held up to the light, it will never be first-class. Better look for a better one. You have to be pretty

37. Zigzag Scallop Fan *(Pecten ziczac Linné)*

severe with yourself, actually, about picking up broken or chipped shells. You'll find better ones, and nobody wants to trade for a broken or chalky number. What's the use, then, of keeping them? Of course if it's a Glory-of-the-Seas Cone or a Prince Cowrie or something like that, all rules are off. Even a nicked one is much to be desired.

It's better to have a lot of small collecting containers than one large one, because fragile shells should be kept separate and not banged around with hardier specimens. The best thing I've seen for carrying shells is a special garment of some kind with pockets. Some are apron-type (like the apron carpenters wear for their nails, only with more and bigger pockets); it hangs around the neck and ties with tape in back. Some others are coat-type, and the pockets are mostly built into the sides below the knees. A lot of women shellers have these.

Hurricanes or near-hurricanes are well publicized, and if you live near a shell beach, you would do well to visit it after such a storm. The majority of the items you'll find then will have the animal inside and be near-perfect. Hurricanes usually come in September when it is warm, so the sea life washed up then ripens rapidly. If you can stand the odors, there are amazing shell collectors' treasures everywhere.

If you've never lived a week or more on a shell beach, you should know what it is like and be prepared. First off, there are a series of pat shell-beach sentences which it might help a newcomer to have translated.

"A very uninteresting (interesting) beach today." This means, "I didn't (I did) find something good."

Similarly, "There's nothing *I* want to pick up." This means the same as the above.

"Tulips (or Nutmegs or anything else) are certainly in today." Just conversation, but impressive. Shows you're in the know.

"A fine beach for miniatures." Same as above.

"I hear they're getting a lot of stuff down by the lighthouse this morning." This means, "I'm afraid you're going to get ahead of me on this stretch, and I'd like to tout you down to the lighthouse area."

"Tomorrow I plan to go up to the west end of the island after breakfast." This means, "I'm heading for the east end of the island at daybreak."

You pretty soon capture the lingo and are tossing off these and others like them with the best of us.

As I've already said, shells motivate everything on such a beach. Conversation always comes around to shells. You go to a restaurant or a hotel for dinner and you find a collection of fine shells in cases along the wall. The hotel may not have them in the dining room but will have a fine collection in or off the lobby. The printed menu will have a shell picture on it.

The women's clothing shops may feature shorts or playsuits made of cloth with some sort of shell design. Shell shops will be everywhere. Not only will these shops have all sorts of shells for sale, but they will sell you (even make for you) shell jewelry, shell novelties.

There will be several boats that advertise dredging expeditions. There will be guides available in smaller boats who will take you wading and collecting in still water.

The motels will all have shells prominently displayed. And these motels will often have a rough table in back of each unit equipped so that you can clean your take. There will be racks for your tools, your acid and Clorox bottles.

At these motels, before it is light, car doors will close, car lights will go on as the shellers in the know make for the part of the beach they think will prove best for them that morning.

There will be, perhaps, a community center of some kind where there will be a fine display of shells. And where the shell club—there will be a shell club, of course—will have its meetings and hold its deliberations.

The shell club will run various events. Some of these will be competitive, with members starting at dawn on a minus tide and collecting for so many hours, and returning to the community house or other designated point at a set time to have their take evaluated. The prizes go to the greatest number of different kinds found, or the best, or both.

The best of these competitive events, and the only ones nationally publicized that I know of, are the Sanibel Shell Fair and the Naples Shell Fair. These are held for three days in February and March each year. Whole collections are entered under various categories, and ribbons are given by the judges to the winning entries. There are concession stands, and it is a gala event, all built around tiny mollusk skeletons. At the 1965 Sanibel Shell Fair, R. Tucker Abbott, one of the world's greatest authorities on malacology, was one of the judges. A Golden Cockle took the grand prize.

On a shell beach nobody walks upright. People's heads are bent forward and they move at a snail's pace. This is called the shellers' stoop. The fingers of those shellers whom you meet and shake hands with are likely to be stained with acid.

There's no night life on a shell beach. You can't stay up late and still beat somebody to that fine stretch of beach in the dawning. There is nobody worrying much about golf or horse racing or movies.

All these customs and institutions that I have described, you may not find on every shell beach. But on each you'll find some of them.

Nonshelling friends ask you, "Whatever do you do?"

It's a pretty hard question to answer. You tell them that you shell the beach, you wade the bay, you do a little skin-diving in deeper water, you work on your shells in the early evening and go to bed early. Even while you're saying it, you know that it doesn't sound like much. But it is. Always providing, that is, that you've been bitten by the shell-collecting bug. It's fascinating. And I for one just can't find anywhere near time enough to do all I want to do. This is a statement I've long since given up trying to explain to the unsympathetic nonsheller.

I'd like it understood here and now that I'm not eccentric

like other shell collectors, and that I don't wear an Outfit in cold weather. I choose simply and tastefully a long-brimmed tuna-fishing cap, a heavy gray leather jacket that comes down below the bottom of my bathing trunks, and a pair of huaraches. When I have these things on, people seem especially friendly; they're always trying to hide a smile when they meet me.

Once when I was out like that I collected three live specimens, and not long afterward I told Marg she'd better check the refrigerator—something seemed to have spoiled. The next day it was worse. We searched under things, looked in corners, quartered the living room, noses twitching, like a bird dog quartering a stubble field. The odor seemed to surround us.

I finally thought of the leather jacket. In the pocket there were those specimens that had once been alive but definitely no longer were. Marg claims I forgot them, but I know some enemy must have sneaked them back into the pocket when I wasn't looking. I removed these shells to a point roughly half a mile from the cottage, and my family were speaking to me again in almost no time. Even this incident has been a nice conversation piece.

There are, all in all, a lot of people being busy on a shell beach. One woman said to me, "Every find is a joy. If it ever ceases to be, shelling wouldn't be fun any more." And there is a lot of competition; there are moments of excruciating triumph when you find That Shell.

There are exercise and sunshine, beautiful sunrises and gorgeous sunsets, and just quiet contentment.

At Island Inn they say, "The shellers go to bed at nine. The hellers stay up till nine-thirty."

It's a pretty basic life. It sounds dull, probably, to someone who doesn't like shells.

10

Shallow-Water Collecting

COMPLETELY different from beach collecting is the shallow-water collecting of live mollusks. On the flats you find only the more sophisticated collectors, never the by-the-day people who are looking only for pretty shells. And as a result, on the flats there never seems to be the competition that you find on the beach.

To begin with, the fact that the shells you are looking for are seldom in plain sight, and that when you make finds they have to be processed extensively, accounts for some of this, of course.

Here again, the tide table is indispensable, especially if you have never shelled the area before. You need very definitely to know whether you can expect more or less water on a flat you contemplate wading. And, just as in beach shelling, you need the tide tables for purposes of planning. Here, too, a low tide is desirable, and a minus tide is something to know about and prepare for days in advance.

The minus tide comes when the moon, which exerts the most influence on the sea, and the sun, which exerts a lesser influence, are both exerting that influence in the same line at the same time. The U. S. Coast and Geodetic Survey in Washington, D.C. will furnish you a tide table for less than a dollar. Or, on shell beaches, some enterprising merchant usually gets out a tide table with his advertising on it, which he gives gratis. This is the best bet if you can find such a service, because it gives only information about the area where you are staying, and never has to be "translated."

In beach shelling, about all you really need is an outfit to keep you warm or covered, and a container to carry shells. In shallow-water shelling you need equipment.

Every sheller has his own methods; some wade carrying everything they might foreseeably need (which is an awful lot), and some go with a minimum, things with which you cannot for practical reasons dispense.

The first, and to my mind the most important, "must" is a pair of heavy-soled sneakers. Under no circumstances, up to and including extreme poverty, should you wade the flats barefoot. Oyster shells have sharp edges; barnacles on barely submerged pieces of waterlogged wood would make a butcher's knife look like a dull weapon. Sea urchins, a pincushion with the sharp ends out, have spines that can cause a painful wound, can break off in your flesh and require a visit to a doctor if deeply imbedded. Stupid people still break bottles and throw the jagged pieces out onto mud flats. Stingrays manage to work themselves into sand or mud so that only a little hump containing their head and eyes is visible, and there they wait. In clear water, they can see you coming and they dart away in plenty of time. In roily water it might be possible to step on one. They have a stinger on the tail (but not on the end; back toward the body) which they would then try to whip around and into your leg. This is a hypodermic-needle-type thing and injects poison. The poison, depending on circumstances and the size of the ray, can be lethal. A friend of mine received such a wound, collapsed and was rushed to the hospital. She remained there several days, then she and her husband traveled on by car. But sitting in the car for long hours cut off the circulation enough so that on the way north she again had to be entered in a hospital. People have died when they could not be quickly attended.

I do not say these things to frighten anyone; it would be doing nobody a favor to pass off as nothing what is potentially a very real danger to your life. Potentially, because the danger can be cut down almost to nothing if you will take one precaution.

When you are wading in water roily enough so that you think a stingray would have trouble seeing you coming, slide your feet rather slowly along the bottom instead of picking them up and setting them down.

The sliding insures that your feet will first touch the outstretched wings or the tail or head. (A ray looks more like some horrible bird without a neck than it does like a fish.) This gives the ray a chance to spurt away and does not pin him down the way stepping on him would. Only when he is pinned down or banged into solidly does he use the stinger.

I have read that wading in trousers or slacks will protect you against the sting of a stingray. I cannot advise you forcefully enough not to put your faith in such protection. It won't protect your leg any more than trousers would protect you against a knife thrust or the jab of a hypodermic needle. Wearing trousers or slacks is a fine protection against the floating hairlike tentacles of the Portuguese man-of-war that will raise red welts wherever they touch your flesh and that burn like a line of acid. They will protect you, too, from various vegetation types that might poison you. But they won't protect against the stingray. True, the heavy-soled sneakers won't protect you either, directly, but they make sliding your feet possible, and that in turn makes you safe.

My second "must" is clothing to protect yourself from the sun, especially if your tan is not yet perfect. You know enough to protect yourself from usual sunburn. But the trouble comes next to the water line, between shorts or rolled-up trousers and the water itself. Somehow people ignore those inches and suffer tortures as a result. The salt water wets, then dries, that area of skin over and over, and this increases the burn. Better leave the slacks on and rolled down if your legs are lily-white. The back of your neck is another danger area. Usually you walk upright but with your head bent forward; that leaves the back of your neck flat and stretched.

The next "must" is some sort of digging tool. Some people use an Army-surplus small folding shovel; in fact one motel I stayed at furnished one of these with each room. Some use a clam hoe of the Cape Cod type. Some use a trowel. But you'll need something because your fingernails will neither do the job nor stand the punishment.

The last real "must" is something in which to carry your take. It can be just a few solid-cloth bags, or mesh bags, or plastic bags, or one of the fancy items mentioned in the preceding chapter. Small jelly jars with screw-on covers which fit into your pocket or into one of the bags will keep fragile or live items separate from others.

There are plenty of other things that would be helpful, but, in my opinion, these are the basic necessities. In my case, the rest are kept in the trunk of the car, which is usually parked near enough the scene of operations so that if extra equipment is needed I can walk over and get it quickly. That method saves a lot of lugging, since some things you'd use only once or twice a year.

If there is water on the flat, in quantity greater than a few inches, a "near-must" is some sort of watertight glass frame that can be forced a little below the surface and that you can look through to see the bottom clearly. Even during a flat calm, there is enough movement of the surface, with resultant shadows and blurring, that it is very difficult to see exactly. The glass clears all that up and miraculously you can see about as clearly as you could in the air. Until you have experienced this it is hard to believe.

The glass can be fitted into one side of a wooden frame and made watertight by caulking. Or it can be one of the glass-bottom buckets which are sold commercially, or (least bulky of all to carry) a pair of skin-diver's goggles. You don't need to wear these, only press them against the water surface and look down through them.

If you are working in cold water, you can become very uncomfortable after an hour or two of wading. Too much of this can even be a health hazard over a period of days or weeks. And so I use a pair of fishermen's waders, which come to my armpits and are held up with suspenders. I own them for fishing anyway, and so I keep them in the car trunk. They have a large inside pocket in front, up next to the top, which comes in very handy for carrying small tools, jars, and even the shells themselves. And they have very heavy rubber boot-type bottoms which are a fine protection against everything.

Another "near-must" is a pair of gloves of some sort; cheap, heavy work gloves are fine. True, you can get along without these, with extreme care, but there is so much that could cut your fingers or otherwise hurt your hands, and gloves take up so little room, that it is well to use them whenever you do any but the most routine picking up. Barnacles, which may be on any shell, are actually the greatest source of hand cuts.

If you're planning to shell at night, you need a flashlight or an electric lantern. It's always a good idea to have a jackknife with you. Hundreds of emergency situations can arise that can only be handled with some sort of knife. If you live on the Pacific Coast or in rocky areas anywhere, a hammer and chisel in the car will allow you to take an abalone shell if you can't slide the knife blade under quickly. The same is true of chitons, limpets, and other rock-clinging creatures. It is well, too, to have a crowbar or a smaller wrecking bar in the car if you are to work in territory where there might be rocks to pry or turn over. As you get more and more into the thing, you'll find many other refinements, things that can be carried constantly in the trunk of the car against the hour when you need them.

As we have seen in the previous chapters, mollusks buried in the sand or mud in the majority of cases stretch their siphon or siphons up to clean water. But they are very sensitive, and the jarring of the ground anywhere near them will cause them to retract the siphons below the surface and possibly into the shell.

You therefore have to move slowly and with extreme caution if you are to see these appendages and locate the mollusk in that manner. When the siphon is retracted the water is forced out. In the case of some clams, when the place they are hiding is entirely out of water, this action causes a spurt of water that will go a foot or two into the air. This is a dead giveaway. Go to that spot, and you will find the siphon hole. Dig beside it. You dig beside it instead of directly down above it so that you won't risk harming the shell with the shovel's edge. Then you can take the animal with your hands from the side of the hole you have dug.

In the same way tracks in the mud or sand can be just as helpful to the collector. Each animal makes a distinctive track. As you collect, you will find out by observation or by asking to be shown by those who know, which mollusk makes which track. The more of this information you can acquire, the better success you will have wading.

In the same way, the holes made by the siphons of mud-living mollusks are likely to be different one from the other. Sometimes the difference, which would be mainly in shape and size, is very marked. Sometimes your eye has to be extremely sharp to detect a difference. Learning these differences will pay off handsomely.

If, in spite of your best efforts at moving gently, there are no siphons and no squirts of water to help you, you'll have only these holes to guide you. And to save time, there is one hole you should learn quickly. That is the fiddler-crab hole. These fiddlers are no good to you (unless you are a sheepshead fisherman), and you can waste a great deal of time digging into their very inviting, relatively large holes until you learn to avoid them. Furthermore, if you do dig into them and reach down bare-handed to pick out the hard brown body under the impression it is a shelled mollusk, you are likely to suffer a good healthy pinch from the efficient crab claw which this small crustacean sports.

If you hope to get the delicate-shelled Angel Wing (*Barnea costata Linné*) from the flats, you will have to be a fast digger. In soft mud the Angel Wing can dig about as fast as you can, and he will keep right on going to avoid you until he strikes something solid. In sandy areas he can't go quite that fast. The Razor Clam is another that could give pointers to a gopher.

If an Angel Wing is a possibility on your expedition, carry a bucket with you that will hold sea water. The Angel Wing has a tremendous siphon, as I have said, that will not fit inside the shell. Yet this mollusk contracts so violently in an effort to get as much as possible inside that often the shell is broken. You have killed a mollusk and still have nothing to show for your blisters. If you put him in salt water as soon as you pull him out of the hole, often actually pulling him by his siphon, the contracting will not be that severe. Occasionally one will contract and break his shell just in trying to escape you.

Since an Angel Wing digs so deep, and since its water spurt is probably your best means of locating it, mark the place with your eye. And when you get there insert a stick into the hole as a guide to the direction the animal took.

Beds of Purple Olives (*Olivella biplicata Sowerby*), a gorgeous shell, are a possibility on the lower Pacific coastal area. The King's Crown Conch (*Melongena corona Gmelin*) is, like the Angel Wing, one you will want to collect live because beach-collected specimens are almost always imperfect. And whereas a beach-collected Angel Wing either will be without the little "ear" inside or will be a single valve or both, similarly the King's Crown will have had the sharp pointed spikes in its crown dulled by rolling and bumping until the specimen is worthless. If you are lucky you'll find the King's Crown on a hunting expedition and capture him easily. Failing this, you'll need to trail one or distinguish

38. Lettered Olives (*Oliva say-ana Ravenel*)

39. Baby's Ears or Lady's Ears (*Sinum perspectivum Say*)

the points of his shell just protruding from the sand. They are hard to recognize because they look like the sharp edges of an oyster shell.

The track of the Lady's Ear (*Sinum perspectivum Say*) is wide and distinctive. You can follow it and dig out the animal. Remember, it is just like a glob of gelatin and the small delicate shell is completely inside this glob. Here again, once you know what the track looks like, collecting becomes easy.

Even when specimens are in plain sight, you won't always be able to see them. The periostracum of even some beautiful shells is drab and blends in with the background or the vegetation. Shells may be barnacle encrusted, mud-covered, even have green slime encasing them, or be hidden in beds of green slimelike vegetation. Arks are likely to be in these thick vegetation areas, which are uncovered only during a minus tide. You'll find murex shells there, too, and star shells. Simnia snails can be taken sometimes on sea fans.

Some collectors carry a small stiff brush to get through the gook on the outside of the shells they collect, enough to see whether or not that particular specimen is worth taking home. And if pools remain on the flats at low tide, it is often worthwhile just to stand quietly a long time and look into them. Siphons may reappear; you may see something you had taken for a rock, move. What looked like a glob of growth may turn out to be a cowrie covered completely by its mantle. The longer you stand there and look, the more you are likely to see. In fact I would be willing to wager that there will be at least one obvious item which you'll astonish yourself by suddenly seeing after you had been looking right at it for some time.

Mollusks, especially bivalves, are often found in beds for breeding and propagation purposes, good food conditions, or other reasons. Find one and you will find others. Learn these bed locations, and you will be able to go back when you need another specimen of that particular mollusk for trading.

Before we leave the flats we should mention again the Geoduck or "Gooeyduck" (*Panope generosa Gould*). As its Latin name suggests, this bivalve is a whopper. And in the northern Pacific states where it is found, it is considered a fine addition to the family menu. This clam will weigh one side or the other of a dozen pounds, so that a successful capturing of one of these is a financial item to the lucky hunter. Three a day per person are allowed.

However, this doesn't bode as ill for the species as you might think, since they are found outside the usual low-tide line. Only on a minus tide, then, are they reasonably procurable. Since there are only two, possibly three, days each month of minus tide, and since these come in daylight hours only in the summer, it isn't as easy as it might seem to get a meal of Gooeyduck.

The mollusk himself doesn't help matters any; he can go down about as deep as the Angel Wing. Even if you are sure the hole you are digging around is a Gooeyduck hole, you still have plenty of work. For this the stovepipe technique is recommended by hunters in the know. You dig a foot or more till the hole starts to fill, then jam a length of stovepipe into it. One operator keeps working the stovepipe farther down and the other bails sand and water frantically until, if all goes well, you can get hold of the neck of the Gooeyduck and pull him up through the stovepipe.

Those who don't subscribe to the stovepipe technique or who can't make it work have to make a man-sized excavation next to the hole, and keeping this bailed out enough to work in is a pretty energetic task, what with the pail bumping against the shovel and two people into each other. All in all a Gooeyduck hunter earns his meat.

Add to that the fact that the mollusk is definitely not as tender as prime filet mignon and you escalate the problems. The mantle is sliced for frying; and the siphon, which will stretch out to nearly three feet and accounts for more than half the weight of the animal, is cut up for chowder or stew. The flavor is elegant, and Gooeyducking is a way of life on the Pacific Northwest coast.

If you are walking a flat at minus tide, and to reach an island you would have to wade a depression from it or a point of land, make very sure you are not so intent on your shelling that you are caught out there by the incoming tide ripping through the low area fast enough and deep enough so that you can't wade back. If you don't know the area, be sure to make inquiries about rips and undertows and find out, before you venture away from dry land, what is safe and what isn't.

If you are wading where there are coral reefs exposed at low or minus tide, you need to take extra precautions. Many things dangerous to man grow on or hide in crevices in coral. Don't reach into crevices that you can't see into. Avoid stepping into vegetation on the coral for fear this might hide a hole or something worse. Best not wade bare-legged here because coral could scrape or cut your ankles. And always be particularly careful of your footing. In the Pacific the Giant Clam is often embedded in coral, with vegetation around and even in the opening. And to step into that opening inadvertently would be disaster.

Where there are rocks or ledges in your wading plans, as there are in New England and along much of the Pacific Coast, you will need to turn over loose rocks and wedge others apart. Your wrecking bar comes in handy here. You'll expose all sorts of shelled mollusks with this strategy. Probably if a rock ledge is at all uneven there will be pools of water left. In an area like Maine's coast, these rock pools produce a great variety. If you wade an area that is under a foot or two of water, you may find that floating over it in a rowboat or canoe will allow you to see more siphons; you won't be jarring the ground this way. Better still, if the water is warm enough, there are skin-diving boards available which have a piece of glass set into the bottom in such a position that you can look through it as you lie face down upon it. This not only shows you more siphons, it also allows you to see the bottom clearly without the fuss of a glass-bottom pail.

Remember, too, when you are wading in several feet of water, that the octopus lies in crevices; look for the debris of his living to warn you of his presence. And remember that although a Carrier Shell looks like a small pile of used shells, don't be so eager to collect this hard-to-find specimen that you grab without investigating. The sea urchin tries to camouflage himself on a purely temporary basis with old shells, and to grab such a pile without caution and find a sea urchin underneath could give you a nasty wound.

You will probably find that night collecting on the flats in just ordinary tide conditions is many times more productive than daytime wading. Each mollusk has his own habits and feeding times. A great many species available to the wader begin to appear half an hour or so after the tide has turned and started in. Many of them hunt only at night. They remain under rocks and in their hiding places in the daytimes. Cowries are hard to find in the open any time except at night. Some mollusks feed just as morning breaks. Some feed at an exact time in the tide cycle.

Some mollusks appear at certain times of the year only, probably because of water temperature or breeding or other migration. In a place like Key West, Florida, the water is too warm in the summer for successful wading; the mollusks don't like it that warm, and those that are able to do so go to deeper water.

If you are after very small shells, instead of trying to hunt them and pick them up singly from the bottom or from between rocks with forceps or tweezers, many collectors build themselves a sieve, just a wooden square with copper screening across the bottom. Mud from the likely areas can be screened through this and real treasures found. If you're going to remain only a day or two in a particular place or are traveling by plane or train, just a piece of screening without the frame will work nicely.

I have told you that in beach shelling you should take what you can get when you can get it; those shells may not be in again. In shallow-water shelling, when you come upon beds, *exactly the opposite is true.*

Take only what you need for your own collection and for any trades you may have on the fire at the moment. The bed will be there; you can return for others if and when you need them. Dig a selection, look them over, take the best for your needs and *put the others back carefully.* This goes, too, for species that are not found in beds.

Such a course is to your advantage and to the advantage of all shell collectors in several ways. First, it preserves the supply of that animal to breed. Breeding will replace those you have taken. You will not be a party to wiping out a species as the carrier pigeons and the herds of buffalo were once wiped out. To be sure, this is a smaller thing, but an Angel Wing, for instance, is still a species of animal. If you clean out every bed you find, and everybody else cleans out every bed he finds, the species will become extinct. Pricewise, this will do you no good because there will be so many of them glutting the market in the process that the price will be next to nothing. And the trading value will be the same.

A story is told on one of the Gulf Coast keys in Florida about a bed of Angel Wings that was extensive. The shell guides took people there and allowed each person one or two. And when a shell collector or native needed a trading item or a quick dollar, he would take a few. The bed stayed about the same.

But someone decided to make a killing. He dug up the whole bed completely, some say by mechanical means. The supply was huge, the price broke to pennies so that his profits never materialized, and the best bed on the island was gone for all time.

On the beach, the shells you find are dead or will die. Take all you can carry if you can use them. But when you are collecting live, take only a few and keep the various species available to yourself and others always.

Shallow-water collecting, then, up to shoulder depth, is very productive of finer specimens than can be found with less trouble on the beach. Those who practice the art are the more advanced collectors. They watch the tide tables carefully and make their plans accordingly, especially when there is an extra low or minus tide. Low tide lasts about fourteen minutes in most places, but the collector can operate effectively for an hour each side of that. Night collecting is more productive than daylight collecting, but also more trouble. You should take only a few specimens to preserve the various species. All sorts of equipment is useful and can be held in reserve in the car trunk, but only heavy-soled sneakers, a shovel or hoe, sunburn-proof clothing and items in which to carry your shells are absolutely necessary.

11

Deep-Water Collecting

A LOT of mollusks live in water that is from six feet to several hundred feet in depth. Most of these never see the flats, in fact are never out of water in a lifetime.

I have told you a little about the ones that live at extreme depths, and I mentioned the Paper Nautilus or Argonaut Shell that floats its eggs in a seagoing cradle. In addition there is the Purple Sea Snail (*Janthina janthina* and *Janthina globosa*). This shelled mollusk lives its life as a sailor, and we will examine its fascinating habits and life in more detail later.

On the shelving floor of the ocean there are thousands of species which collectors for centuries were unable to reach. However, shell collectors have adapted skin diving for all depths where they can stand the pressure.

Actually "skin diving" is a misnomer because many divers wear "wet suits" for warmth in cold water. Water gets between the tight rubber-type suit and the skin, and the body heat of the diver warms up this film of water and allows the owner to be fairly comfortable.

He uses watertight goggles, which allow him to see the fascinating underwater world as if it were in air, and he swims along the surface watching that world pass underneath him. He breathes through a "snorkle" which he holds in his mouth. This is a tube that looks like a misshapen letter S. There is a small chamber in the out-of-water end of this snorkle which houses a ping-pong ball. When that end is sticking up out of water the ping-pong ball drops out of the tube mouth by gravity.

But if the diver sees a shell and dives to get it, the instant the water hits that little celluloid ball, the ball is jammed up by its own buoyancy into the tube mouth, blocks it off and keeps water from flooding down into the mouth of the diver. When the end reappears above the surface, the ball again drops out of the opening to allow normal breathing. At first it is difficult for some—at least it was for me—to learn for sure to breathe only through the mouth, but it's amazing how fast a few chokings will teach you.

The shell collector can thus float along in water of reasonable depth, see siphons without disturbing the mollusk and do his shelling in comfort. This takes him one step farther out than floating around on one of those float boards.

The best thing I know of as a floating base of operations for such an expedition is an ordinary round fruit basket set into an inflated inner tube. You attach this to your wrist by a string long enough to reach bottom at any point you plan to explore. The basket holds any tools you may think you will need. And it is the depository for the treasures you hope to find. The inner tube is very buoyant and will hold your whole weight while you rest after each dive if that is necessary. This is a practical and inexpensive outfit, though with tubeless tires more and more coming to be standard equipment on new cars, old patched inner tubes are not as easy to find as they used to be.

All this is not without danger. Care and know-how will practically wipe out the danger, but you should learn what to guard against.

In the first place, in my opinion you should make it a rule never to shell this way alone. There can be cramps or any number of unforeseen occurrences which would be minor annoyances if someone were there to help you but might be fatal if you were alone. Sure, these occurrences are few and far between, but they only have to happen once.

The deeper the water, too, the more likely you are to come face to face with something big in the way of marine life. There are sharks, barracuda, moray eels to think about. You may never see one of them, but still it is a distinct possibility that you will. Mostly they are as afraid of you as you are of them, but if you corner or meet one suddenly you could find yourself in real trouble. Usually you would see such creatures at a distance and avoid a confrontation. But if you were intent on what you were doing, or he was intent on capturing food, he might be suddenly at close quarters.

Barracuda are a very-warm-water fish. They are shaped like a pickerel or northern pike. They have vicious teeth and with these have taken chunks out of people. The person in the wet suit is not very vulnerable. And all skin divers say they have met these fish and been ignored hundreds of time. But still there have been incidents of attack. Some authorities say that the less tan you have, the whiter your flesh, the more chance of attack.

The shark seldom attacks man. Mullet sharks that I'm used to seeing off the Florida coast are big and scary looking, but are not interested in people. But lately the Pacific beaches have had trouble with man-eaters.

I stood once to my waist in roily water landing a sea trout and was just about to succeed when a huge mullet shark surged to the surface within two feet of me and knocked the trout off the hook, made another surge and caught the trout. I was meantime already on my way out of there; that's how you instinctively feel with anything that big that close. But calmer consideration told me that if he had been interested in me instead of the trout he most certainly could have had a fine meal of Hoyt without trouble. It's best to go in the opposite direction when you see anything that big.

The moray eel, too, has vicious teeth, sharp in front and cutting in back. It looks like a snake. It is deadly dangerous when fighting for its life. But most authorities agree that it will attack man only in defense of its home in a rock or other recess. Then it will attack and has been known to fasten onto an arm so determinedly that it had to be pried loose. I've known of one that was thirty pounds in weight, so they are not small creatures. If you see one, just go in the other direction and probably he will too. And never approach a cavern of any sort under water except with the greatest of caution. Not only the moray, but the octopus and any of a number of other villainous-looking items might be lurking there.

There are also big porpoises, manta rays (a fish about the size and shape of your Thanksgiving table), tarpon and other huge nonharmful creatures. One time I was skin diving with a friend from a rowboat and he dove in first. His feet were barely out of sight when his front end came shooting back out of water and he surged over the side of the boat all in one motion. Since he usually had trouble climbing back in, I was astonished. I asked him what happened.

"I was face to face with a huge tarpon."

I said, "But a tarpon won't hurt you."

And he said, "Does *he* understand that?"

In skin diving, operate in deep water in inverse ratio to your age and agility, wear a belt knife, and carry some sort of sharp prod—a spear or gig or just a sharpened metal rod fastened to your wrist with a rope—just in case. Again the main rule: see, then go in the opposite direction but don't turn your back.

For those who want shells that lie even deeper, there are compressed-air tanks which strap onto your shoulders and allow you to stay under a long time exploring a considerable area. Personally this is not for me. I dislike the idea of some mechanical device, perhaps subject to failure, coming between me and the continued easy enjoyment of breathing. If you are planning to get your shells this way, get your advice from a professional. It will be sufficient for me to say that you certainly must never attempt this *without* getting a lot of instruction and advice from a practicing diver, and without first trying out the technique in shallow water.

In skin diving of any sort, success comes from turning

over rocks, pieces of water-logged wood, prying apart other things, examining whatever seems promising, just as we advised in the preceding chapter.

If you want no part of aqua-lung diving, there are other methods for obtaining deeper-water shells. The first and less-known of these is mopping, aptly named because the apparatus used, sometimes called a "tangle," has a lot of the characteristics of a mop.

This instrument is many times the size of an ordinary mop and uses an iron bar for a mop frame. To this iron bar are attached varying lengths of raveled rope or the binder twine used by farmers in some reapers or bailers. A "V" of rope or cable is attached to each end of this rod, and the mop dragged along the bottom by a boat.

This operates on the theory that any bivalve, when a bit of foreign matter suddenly intrudes into the shell opening, will clamp down on it and hold on. It works particularly well for scallops and pen shells. And it will also tangle in the spines of the Thorny Oyster, sometimes called the Chrysanthemum Shell (*Spondylus americanus* on the Atlantic Coast and *Spondylus pictorum* on the Pacific Coast), which is one of the most beautiful and hard-to-believe shells in the world. It is a mollusk both of whose valves are covered with delicately curving spikes or "thorns," some of them quite long. Some are straight, some curved, and the whole gives the effect of the petals of a chrysanthemum. The Pacific variety is more colorful, the Atlantic variety perhaps more delicate. Whole collections have been made of this shell alone. One collection close to Sanibel is in the Marine Museum at Fort Myers, a lovely, colorful display against black. Those who see it are impressed with the shading from white to color and from one color to another, and most of all impressed with the fact that the mantle of a bivalve could have managed to build these calcium spikes of such length. It seems impossible that it could have been done that way. If your mop brings up a perfect specimen of a Thorny Oyster, you will be very lucky indeed.

40. The Thorny Oyster (*Spondylus*) is sometimes called a Chrysanthemum Shell.

The pen shells, as I have already told you, have large valves and on these you are likely to find Boat Shells, Turkey Wings, Jewel Boxes and other shells. So your mop may bring up pens which you probably don't want (unless it

41. Jewel Boxes attached to each other

42. Florida Spiny Jewel Boxes (*Echinochama cornuta Conrad*)

should be the Flesh Pen, a pink shell found in the Florida Keys) but which would give you shells that you do want.

The tangle may also bring you a few univalves which closed on the ropes when, upon feeling it, they hastily pulled in their feet and opercula. You will surely pick up starfish whose arms and their nobs will tangle in the mop (I'll tell you more later about the use of the mop in efforts to rid the oyster industry of these starfish) and many other interesting creatures.

In mopping you need a lot of rope and a release mechanism. There are various release mechanisms but the principle is to have one end hold, the other release under heavy pressure, so that if the mop catches on something immovable on the bottom, you can get your equipment back and reset it to work again.

The other method of getting deep-water shells, time-tried, is the dredge.

There are a number of different types and sizes of dredge, both triangular and rectangular. All that I've seen have had a metal frame, the main part made of heavy mesh screening or fishnet. If fishnet is used for the part that will hold the load, it is usually gathered together at the back and tied with a piece of string so that when it is brought up full, the string can be untied and the take dumped out through that big opening. Metal mesh bodies have to be emptied either through the front or through a door in back with a button on it. If you are using fishnet, this will rip and wear out quickly if the bottom is at all rough, so some kind of metal apron should be dragged under it from the lower rod of the frame to protect it.

The frame itself is usually strap iron, with the lower bar sharpened on the forward side, and set at a slight downward angle to dig into the sand or muck and run it through the screening or the netting. Special irons are run to a single point from the four corners (or three if it is triangular) and the rope from the boat attached at that point. Again, with a dredge there should be some provision made to have one iron arm break away and fold back to release the dredge if it should get caught on something. The simplest release device is just to tie one arm with string which can be broken if need be. There are more elaborate (and expensive) release mechanisms, but the main aim is to see that you don't lose your dredge if it catches on something; dredges are expensive.

The dredge can be towed behind any sort of boat. If you use a rowboat with oars or small outboard motor, the least expensive setup you can choose, you must operate close to shore and will need to pick your day carefully even to do that. If you use a heavier outboard boat you can venture into far deeper water, especially if you have a heavy enough motor to get you back quickly if weather conditions should change without much warning.

Or you can go with a large cabin cruiser or charter boat, and dredge over various far-from-home ocean bottoms and spend one or more nights aboard the cruiser. Usually you'd make for a cove at night if you planned to remain out, and venture forth again the next morning.

You need roughly three times as much rope as you have depth. It is better to err on the side of too much than too little. If you have to have more than 300 or 400 feet of rope (100 feet of water), you'll need weights tied to it to keep it from floating and thus from holding the dredge too high to bite in. If you go in for this in a big way, in water much deeper than 100 or 200 feet (upwards of 400 feet of rope), even weighted five-eights-inch rope will no longer be sufficient, and you will need wire cable. You can bring the rope up by hand from about 150 feet of water, but when you graduate to wire cable you'll need a winch of some sort. Your boat will have to be better equipped.

No matter what size boat you use, you must make some provision for handling what you dump out of the dredge. The best thing I have seen is a humpbacked wooden trough which fits crossways from gunwale to gunwale and sticks out over each of them. You dump the dredge into this trough.

This setup gives the dredging crew a chance to work the take carefully, screen any of it they want to through a fine mesh screen for miniatures, make sure they have everything worth keeping, and then, with a couple of pails of water poured into the trough on each side of the middle hump, flush the remainder over the side. Meantime, with a crew that is big enough, the dredge has long since been put back overside and is being dragged along and thus made ready for pulling up with the next load.

I think perhaps I make this sound a lot easier and more attractive than it really is. In the first place, if it is a very small boat and you are rowing, the whole business is backbreaking. There's not only the rowing, but when this stops there's pulling the heavy dredge up hand over hand while you still try to manage the boat. There isn't room for more than two people while the dredge is coming in, what with that trough or other receptacle. So you'll need to anchor while you sort the take; it requires one to row and one to handle the rope.

But we'll say that you don't row. You yourself are a fine skipper with a fine boat, or you have chartered a cruiser with a man who is, and perhaps he even has a helper. Still there are the smells of the whole operation which could make a glue factory green with jealousy. In fact green is exactly the color these smells are likely to make the faces of all but the oldest hands at the game. The gunk that comes up not only smells bad, it looks bad, especially some of the sponges. And those sorting it get in it pretty near to the armpits. It splashes, gets on your boat, your clothing, and even in your hair. You have to do a good deal of work on yourself to become socially acceptable after a day's dredging. People have told me there are areas where a bucket of gunk from the bottom smells as pure and fresh as the driven snow. I'm glad they found such a place; I never have.

But suppose it doesn't smell too bad and your constitution doesn't rebel. There's still the motion of the boat to add to it. Because of the weight behind and the necessarily very slow forward movement, the boat doesn't take the waves briskly; it wallows. In anything but a dead calm, this motion, added to the sights and odors, will turn your stomach inside out.

Some operators don't screen the gunk right there but fill bags with it and work on it in the evenings at home. Muddy water oozes out from these bags and gets the boat even dirtier than it might otherwise get. It gets unbelievably dirty anyhow. That is why a charter captain charges more to take you dredging for a day than he does to take you sport fishing for the same length of time. He's got to clean the boat after he gets you home. The usual cost is between $60 and $75 for a day. Plus tip.

For this amount of money you may or may not get anything worthwhile. The first time I ever went dredging we got two beat-up dead ark shells and a whole flock of Sand Dollars. These, live, incidentally, are dark greenish-gray and not the grayish-white of the ones you pick up on the beach. I could have walked out onto the beach in front of the cottage, bent over and picked up 100 dead ark shells without moving.

At other times you may feel richly rewarded. But obviously only the very affluent collector is going to be able to dredge often unless he owns his own boat. Dredging from a small boat, where your gasoline is your main expense, cuts down the cost tremendously.

Some people band together to hire a charter boat for dredging and thus cut the individual cost. The problem then is the division of the take. Any way you set this up, some of the party are going to feel that they got the small end of the deal. If this is the only way you can afford a dredging expedition, the best division I know of is to draw lots to get the order, then give the first person everything in the first load, the second everything in the second and so on. This is far from perfect, but other methods are worse. Pooling the cost is never a desirable situation, and you should enter into the plan only with reasonable people whom you know well, never with the ill-tempered of this world.

The better you or the captain knows the bottom, the habits of the mollusks, the shell beds, and navigation in general, the better chance you have that your dredging expedition will prove to be worthwhile. You learn the feel of

43. Ark Shells (*Noetia ponderosa* Say) at left and right; center, Elegant Dosinia (*Dosinia elegans* Conrad)

things, whether the dredge is sliding along or biting in, by trial and error.

And even though blanks are drawn on some of the expeditions, a lot of collectors swear by dredging. This is especially true of the dyed-in-the-byssus addicts. A neighbor of ours at Sanibel a couple of years ago asked her husband to give her for Christmas not a mink coat, not a lovely evening gown or an expensive necklace, but a shell dredge. It is things like this which force me to doff my hat to this wonderful breed apart.

There are several other methods for getting deep-water shells. One of these is from the stomachs of fish. I am told that fish hooked and brought up rapidly from great depths will disgorge, be practically turned inside out by the quick change from great pressure. I have never fished in waters of this depth and so have never seen this first-hand. I do know that some shell collectors have established working agreements with fish-house employees to slit the stomachs of channel bass (redfish), sheepshead and other types that would swallow shelled mollusks, when they dress such fish. Many books and pamphlets mention rare specimens taken from the stomachs of fish. Obviously, for the ordinary collector this method promises little unless he has a friend in the right kind of fish house.

Much more promising is trapping. The simplest trap is just a bag of dead fish or fish dressings tied to a stone and dropped in water shallow enough so that skin diving will allow you to visit the spot the next day or night. If you are in a good location you'll find a number of carnivorous mollusks trying to get at the bag's contents, drawn by the juices from it carried to them by water currents.

There are a great variety of more sophisticated traps. The best bet usually is to use a trap designed by commercial crabbers or lobstermen. You modify it so that the smaller mollusks can enter easily and be held once they do enter. Traps are particularly effective in rocky areas, deep holes or any other location that would be difficult to dredge. In trapping you are, of course, going to get only univalves that eat flesh, not those that exist on plant life. If there are a lot of crabs in the area in which you want to operate, you'll have to find some way to protect the bait so that it will attract but won't be all eaten by interlopers before your mollusks can even get there.

If you yourself can't or don't want to trap for shells, you can cross the palms of commercial trappers, and they will give you the shells that they bring up in their traps. Lobster fishermen, blue-crab men, stone-crab trappers, Key West crawfish men can all help you. Even the natives of the West Indies islands and the Windward and Leeward Islands who set traps for fish bring up shelled mollusks, some of them very rare.

Then, too, there are the trawlers, the net fishermen, and the shrimpers. These men are becoming more and more shell conscious. Seldom now does a fine shell which comes in with the shrimp or the fish get thrown back. The operators love the extra dollars and know too well what is valuable. Just the other day I was in a shell shop when a crewman from a shrimper came in with a lovely Junonia and asked the operator what she would pay him for it.

Of course if you want to collect your own shells yourself, or get them in trade for shells you have collected, you'll consider that buying them from a crabber or a shrimper is akin to cheating at golf. Still, there are people who do both.

We find, then, that you can take shells in deeper water by skin diving, dredging, trapping, mopping, or from the stomachs of fish. Or you can make friends with, or pay, someone who comes upon them in his daily work. Of these methods, dredging is the surest, but can be by far the most expensive.

12

Everyday Shells—Univalves

I HAVE already told you in Chapter 2 about shells which look like their common names. Let us examine now some other everyday shells throughout the world that you will be able to collect yourself or trade for without an immoderate strain on your bank account.

As you begin to get the feel of shelling, you one day suddenly understand the way the various shells fall into families: the olives, the cones, the whelks and many others. People and books have been talking about this all along. But at first you have no knowledge to base understanding on, and so these are all just so many words.

One day, though, after you have seen a lot of shells and have collected a lot of shells, after you have thought shells, talked shells, identified shells, you are amazed to realize that you understand the whole matter fairly completely. You're even slightly provoked at yourself for being obtuse in the beginning. I am going to assume that by now you have reached or are well past such a point.

Even though there are only a relatively few cowries available in the continental United States, these are lovely and interesting shells and you'll want some of them for your collection. Four of these are available on the Florida coast, one is available on the California coast.

The Atlantic Gray Cowrie (*Cypraea cinerea Gmelin*) and the Atlantic Yellow Cowrie (*Cypraea spurca acicularis*

Gmelin) are small, somewhere in the neighborhood of an inch in length. But the other two are larger. The Measled Cowrie (*Cypraea zebra Linné*) is almost three inches long, and the Deer Cowrie (*Cypraea cervus Linné*) is an inch or so larger even than that. Both are spotted and have the usual cowrie shape. But the Measled Cowrie has dots inside its spots. The Measled Cowrie secretes body acid which, when the animal is allowed to deteriorate at all in the shell, is likely to spoil the inside coloring.

The one cowrie on the California coast is the Chestnut Cowrie (*Cypraea spadicea Swainson*), which is in the two-inch class. Even this one isn't very common. It is found in rocky areas from Santa Barbara south.

In addition, there are two other lower-Caribbean cowries, the Panama Cowrie (*Cypraea cervinetta Kiener*) and the Mouse Cowrie (*Cypraea mus Linné*).

But these seven near-home species are only a drop in the bucket to the total available cowries. Cowries are found in the Pacific, the Indian Ocean, the Red Sea, the Mediterranean Sea, and along the African coast. They are found on mainlands and on islands and reefs. Mostly they have that cowrie shape in adult life, rounded on the top and a slit with "teeth" at the bottom. There are literally dozens of kinds.

The most famous one, very common indeed, is the Money Cowrie (*Cypraea moneta Linné*) which we told you about in Chapter 8. Another very common one is the Hump Back or Mourning Cowrie (*Cypraea mauritiana Linné*), which is one of the sturdiest cowries. The Snake Head Cowrie (*Cypraea caputserpentis Linné*) is very common, too. The Ringed, or Gold Ringer, Cowrie (*Cypraea annulus Linné*) is easy to find.

There are a number of cowries named for animals or birds: the Pacific Deer, the Panther, the Tiger, the Tortoise, the Mole, the Camel, the Lynx, the Thrush, the Kitten. The Map Cowrie (*Cypraea mappa Linné*) and the Stolid Cowrie (*Cypraea stolida Linné*) are a couple of the most popular

44. Snake-Head Cowrie (*Cypraea caputserpentis Linné*)

among collectors, but these are much less common. In addition there are several cowries which we'll speak of in the chapter on rare shells. The easy ones you should be able to get; finding *any* of the harder ones at all is just gravy for a United States collector.

45. Tiger Cowries (*Cypraea tigris Linné*), front and back

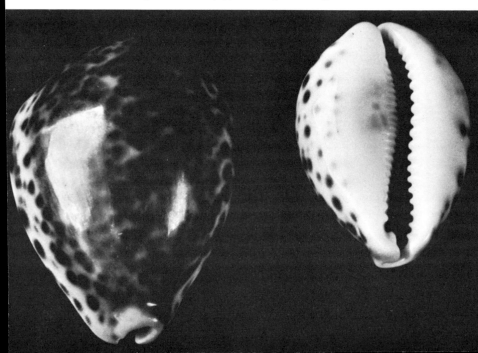

46. At top, Tiger's Eyes, (*Natica canrena Linné*), sometimes called Cat's Eyes and sometimes Atlantic Natica, next below are Florida Cones, (*Conus floridanus Gabb*); next the Sailor's Ear, (*Labiosa plicatella Lamarck*); under that the Pen Shell, (*Atrina rigida Solander*). On the sides are a border of double cockles, most of them Prickly Cockles (*Trachycardium egmontianum Shuttleworth*).

The cones are another huge family, very abundant in tropical waters. The United States mainland has a long list of interesting cones, but the amazing thing is that of this whole common list, only one comes from our Pacific Coast. That one is the California Cone (*Conus californicus Reeve*), a small cone with a bluish-white central band on brownish-yellow. However, it has a periostracum which changes the color that you see in the live shell.

On the Atlantic Coast there is a fine assortment, a few fairly common, some much harder to get. Of these I've already mentioned the Chinese Alphabet Cone (*Conus spurius atlanticus Clench*), which is found, but pretty rarely, on Gulf of Mexico beaches.

Three others are in this same class: the Florida Cone (*Conus floridanus Gabb*); its darker counterpart, the Dark

Florida Cone (*Conus floridanus floridensis Sowerby*), which has marking; and the Mouse Cone (*Conus mus Hwass*), which is found along our southeast coast on flats.

Most of the others are named *for* somebody—Stimpson's Cone, Jasper Cone, Sozon's Cone, Julia's Cone—and though some of them are probably as common as those I've mentioned, they come mostly in deeper water and are acquired most easily by dredgers. Some of these cones, too, are very rare in the United States but are common in areas of the West Indies where the waters are even warmer.

In the rest of the world, cones are plentiful and interesting both in color and shape. And, as I have already warned, on your world tour you had best not pick up cones in the Pacific because some of them can sting and have in the past killed people. The proper way to pick up any cone that you are not sure of is by the sides, with the palm of your hand opposite the opening, never over it. No part of your hand or body should ever be anywhere where the stinger could be thrust out and jabbed into it.

Of these, the Pacific Lettered Cone (*Conus litteratus Linné*) is the one I see most often; many of these were brought back to this country by the men who fought in the Pacific in World War II. The Leopard Cone (*Conus leopardus Röding*) looks a little like it but grows larger and has a more raised apex.

All these are spectacular, but the Marble Cone (*Conus marmoreus Linné*) and the Hebrew Cone (*Conus ebraeus Linné*) are the most beautiful of the common Pacific Ocean or Indian Ocean varieties. It is hard, though, to pick the best because all of them are lovely.

The Textile Cone (*Conus textile Linné*) is a fairly common shell, but it is much prettier than it acts, being one of the stingers. It is marked with a checked pattern, and perhaps its greatest bid for fame is not the number of people it has killed or made ill but the fact that it is sometimes mistaken for the Glory-of-the-Seas Cone. Its sides, though, are much more rounded.

West Africa has some beautiful cones and one of the common ones is the Butterfly Cone *(Conus papilionaceus Hwass)*. Incidentally, the largest living cone is a West African one, the Prometheus Cone *(Conus prometheus Hwass)*, and this runs to a length of twelve inches. The price averages better than $1 an inch.

Japan, too, has various varieties, the commonest one being Fulmen's Cone *(Conus fulmen Reeve)*. The Austral Cone *(Conus australis Holten)* is another that looks enough like the Glory-of-the-Seas to raise the hopes of some searchers high until they get the sad news that luck has not smiled their way. There are, too, half a dozen varieties of cones available on the Pacific side of Mexico and Central America, if your travels take you in that direction.

The average collector, then, can easily acquire cones, and perhaps, as with the cowries, he can acquire a lot. The really top collectors, on the other hand, have shells like the Prince Cowrie and the Glory-of-the-Seas Cone to shoot at.

Conchs, too, are worldwide. But in this case some of the best and most interesting come from our own area. The Fighting Conchs *(Strombus alatus Gmelin* and *Strombus pugilis Linné)* are the easy ones to collect. They grow to three inches and are obtainable on all south Florida beaches. Most casual collectors never realize that there are two Fighting Conchs, the West Indian *(Strombus pugilis)* and the Florida *(Strombus alatus)*. The rule of thumb on these two is that if the top of the lip slopes up it is the West Indian, and if it slopes down it is the Florida. There are other recognition points that make identification sure, but the up or down turn of the lip top will usually tell you.

The Queen Conch *(Strombus gigas Linné)* is a huge thing, about a foot long. Its lip flares way out, and rises at the lip top higher than the apex. The young of the species do not have the widely flaring lip and for that reason are called rollers. The Queen Conch is used as food, the meat eaten plain or in various kinds of stew or chowder. Florida backwater natives used to be called "conchs" and still are to a lesser degree; the original term was "conch eaters" and this was shortened to just plain "conchs." So enthusiastic has been the acceptance of the Queen Conch as an eatable item that what was once a very common shell is now somewhat rare in Florida. But it is still very plentiful in the West Indies.

There are several other Caribbean conchs, and all of them have that flaring lip and upswing at its top. None of them, though, to the extent of the Rooster Conch (*Strombus gallus Linné*), which really carries this characteristic to the extreme. On top of the up-flaring shoulder there is a narrow half tube which carries that shoulder point about half the shell's length above the apex. This species isn't going to do much rolling end over end, that's certain.

The Milk Conch (*Strombus costatus Gmelin*), one of these Caribbean numbers, is interesting because it has a dwarf counterpart about half its own size in Lake Worth, near Palm Beach.

California has no plentiful member of the true conchs,

47. Milk Conch (*Strombus costatus Gmelin*)

but Hawaii has a very common one in the Spotted Conch (*Strombus maculatus Sowerby*), which is a cream-colored shell with spots of brown. There are a couple of others not so easily come by.

The Indo-Pacific area of the world has a number of conchs and several of them have interesting characteristics. Several have that high shoulder on the lip, and some even have a sort of spike sticking up from it. There are the Bubble Conch (*Strombus bulla Röding*), the Diana's Ear Conch (*Strombus aurisdianae Linné*), the Dog Conch (*Strombus canarium Linné*). The Little Bear Conch (*Strombus urceus Linné*) has some specimens with a black ring around the mouth like a boy who has eaten several chocolate bars. And the Blood-mouth Conch (*Strombus luhuanus Linné*) has an aperture which no dentist should ever show his customers.

One conch which will make an enviable showing in your collection is the Spider Conch. There are nine species, and all of them are from warm waters in the Indo-Pacific area. The reason they are such conversation pieces is that they have appendages which look shudderingly like a huge spider's legs.

The Common Spider Conch (*Lambis lambis Linné*) is the commonest of all and can be purchased for just over a quarter. The biggest is the Giant Spider Conch (*Lambis truncata Humphrey*), which is also common as Spider Conchs go, but would still cost several dollars. The one that produces the biggest shudders in me personally is the Arthritic Spider Conch (*Lambis arthritica Röding*). If your hand is near it when you turn on the light at night, it can give you quite an emotional setback.

So you can see that the conchs offer a challenge to you, but give you a lot of species you should have no trouble finding, and many which because of that huge lip and high shoulder on it, and because of the large size of the shells in general, would make spectacular additions to any collection.

The volutes are another big family that offers almost as much challenge to the collector as those families I've already mentioned. Among volutes there are only a few that aren't at least uncommon, some because they are deep-water dwellers and are brought to the surface mostly by dredging. We have a number of volutes off our East Coast and only one off our West Coast, and that one is not at all common. It is Stearns' Volute (*Arctomelon stearnsi Dall*) and is found mostly up around Alaska.

Among our East Coast and Caribbean volutes, none is common; the Music Volute (*Voluta musica Linné*) comes the nearest. This is a fairly spectacular item if you can get it. In the rest of the world the Philippine Bat Volute (*Aulica vespertilio Linné*) is a common shell, a beauty, and one to strive for. The Philippines also give us a gorgeous crown-spiked ten-inch volute called the Imperial Volute (*Volutocorona imperialis Solander*), which is not common but is low-priced as volutes go.

The uncommon to rare ones, which I'll mention because there are so few common ones, are Kiener's Volute, Dohrn's Volute, Schmitt's Volute, plus a shell with the delightful name of Dubious Volute. And the Junonia which I've talked a great deal about. Each of these has the Latin designation Scaphella, plus exactly the second name you'd expect from those common names.

In the rest of the world there are many gorgeous volutes, some of them large and imposing. Japan has several. There are the Notable Volute (*Fulgoraria concinna Broderip*), which has a large flaring mouth, and the Delicate Volute (*Saotomea delicata Fulton*), a typical volute shape but with vertical ridges. On Taiwan and the Chinese coast there is a very lovely shell named the Flame Volute (*Fulgoraria rupestris Gmelin*). Specimens of these three can be had for under $40. Then, too, there is the shell with the delightful name of Shin-bone Volute (*Teramachia tibiaeformis Kuroda*), which looks more like an auger than a volute. It is worth better than $25.

As you will have noted by this time, the volutes don't always have the same first Latin name, as do the cowries and

48. Ethiopian Volute (*Melo aethiopicus Linné*)

the cones and others. This setup makes the identification and collection of volutes a bit harder than other classifications. At least one catalog (*Van Nostrand's Standard Catalog of Shells*) lists all species under *Voluta*, and then puts these standard designations which I have given in parentheses.

Among the big showy volutes are the Mammal Volute (*Livonia mammilla Sowerby*), sometimes called the False Melon Shell, which is a ten-inch job with a wide lip and large opening. It is used by natives, along with the even larger Ethiopian Volute (*Melo aethiopicus Linné*) and the Indian Volute (*Melo melo Solander*), which are shaped somewhat the same, for bailing out boats. They hold the rounded part of the shell and with a back-hand motion scrape the lip along the bottom of the boat.

In West Africa the Elephant's Snout Volute (*Cymbium cymbium Linné*) rivals the Ethiopian Volute in size at up to fourteen inches. These are all available for under $5; nowhere can you get as much volute for your money as in these big spectacular shells.

The challenge to a collector in the volutes, then, comes from the fact that with a few exceptions they are deep-water shells collected mostly through dredging, and are rare and expensive.

The murex shells are a spiny group and present endless opportunities. Unlike the volutes, many, many murex shells are very common in both this country and the rest of the world, and easily collected. In the United States, murex shells are nowhere near as common on the West Coast as they are on the East and Gulf coasts. However, there are a number of fine murex shells to be had in the Lower California area of Mexico, and there are others in the West Indies below Florida.

The Lace Murex (*Murex florifer Reeve*) you will recognize immediately once you have learned the murex shape. This is one of the most common, along with the Apple Murex (*Murex pomum Gmelin*), which has short spines and is a rounded, tough little shell. They are so plentiful along the Gulf Coast that they wash up frequently, and even perfect live-gathered specimens with opercula are worth only about a nickel.

The Rose Murex (*Murex recurvirostris rubidus F. C. Baker*) is a beautiful little red shell, with a fairly long siphonal canal; it is about as common as the other two. Even the Giant Eastern Murex (*Murex fulvescens Sowerby*), which is a deeper-water shell, is so often brought to the surface by the shrimp boats because of its spines that it is worth only a fraction of a dollar.

On the California coast the Three-winged Murex (*Murex trialatus Sowerby*), the Gem Murex (*Murex gemma Sowerby*), the Santa Rosa Murex (*Murex santarosana Dall*), are all common enough to be worth only in the neighborhood of $1, and the Festive Murex (*Murex festivus Hinds*) can be had for less than half of that.

In the rest of the world the most interesting murex to me is the Venus Comb (*Murex tririmus Perry*) which I have mentioned earlier. This is found in the Indo-Pacific area. This shell, with its almost incredible comb-teeth, is not a terribly expensive shell. And a larger Japanese version (*troscheli*) and a Caribbean version available to United States collectors (*cabriti*) are even less expensive.

The second "must" murex from other areas is the Dye Murex from the Mediterranean (*Murex brandaris Linné*). This was the one that changed the course of colonization and even of history. Therefore, it is a conversation piece for any collection. Even if you cannot collect it yourself or trade for it, the cost to you would be less than half a dollar, well worth the money to any collector for the exciting events which it represents.

There are many other murex shells, of course, only a few of which are, to my mind, special. One of these, the Pink-mouthed Murex (*Murex erythrostoma Swainson*), is not very rare, and I'd recommend it to you because of its delicate coloring. It is found on the Pacific Coast from Mexico south. The Snipe's Bill Murex (*Murex haustellum Linné*) from the Indo-Pacific has a very long siphon canal which rivals that of the Venus Comb, and which gives this shell a long tail. The mantle of the Scorpion Murex (*Murex scorpio Linné*) reaches out and dissolves the old spines as it grows. According to some authorities it may even use the material for keeping the spines at the edge of the lip large and in A-1 condition.

Olives are lovely and gracefully shaped shells. They have an amazingly glossy finish, like polished marble. And they are plentiful.

On our West Coast the Purple Dwarf Olive (*Olivella biplicata Sowerby*) is abundant during months that have warm water, and is easy to find. The same area boasts two others, the Beatic Dwarf Olive (*Olivella baetica Carpenter*) and the San Pedro Olive (*Olivella pedroana Conrad*). On the East Coast the Lettered Olive (*Oliva sayana Rav-*

enal) is very common from the Carolinas clear to Mexico. The Florida keys and the West Indies have the Netted Olive (*Oliva reticularis Lamarck*), which is almost as common. There are several Dwarf Olives (*Olivella*) on the East Coast, too. Thus no collection needs to be without olive specimens.

In the rest of the world there are many varieties of olive shells. Common on the Pacific side of Central America is the Tent Olive (*Oliva porphyria Linné*), which has tentlike markings if you lay the shell flat. In the Indo-Pacific region there is the Orange-mouthed Olive (*Oliva sericea Röding*), which has a variety of markings on the outside, and the Purple-mouthed Olive (*Oliva episcopalis Lamarck*). These two are very plentiful and you should be able to get specimens. The Gibbose Olive (*Oliva gibbosa Röding*) from the Indian Ocean area is very beautiful.

The whelks are common shells, easily collected, especially by residents of the eastern part of the United States. Unlike many mollusks, some of the whelks thrive in cold water. Some are very large and showy.

The Common Northern Buccinum (*Buccinum undatum Linné*) is a cold-water, north Atlantic whelk, and the New England Neptune (*Neptunea decemcostata Say*) is a common shell which is available from Canada south as far as Rhode Island.

Then from the tip of Cape Cod south to New Smyrna, Florida, you will find the Knobbed Whelk (*Busycon carica Gmelin*) and the Channeled Whelk (*Busycon canaliculatum Linné*). These can be big shells, running from five to nine inches. From the Carolinas to Texas and beyond grow the Pear Whelk (*Busycon spiratum Lamarck*) and the commonest of all, the one everybody counts among his first-collected shells, the Left-handed Whelk (*Busycon contrarium Conrad*). This is also called the Lightning Whelk and grows to fifteen or sixteen inches. The *contrarium* describes it. It is *the* one of the few shells that have the opening on the left as you hold the shell in front of you. And so a right-handed Left-handed Whelk is a rarity indeed, and quite valuable.

If you can find one of these, then usually it is not difficult to find a regular specimen of about the same size and markings since the species is so common. These two, displayed together, are a triumph.

The young Pear Whelks and the young Left-handed Whelks have much the same look before they get their full growth. Many times I have thought I had a right-handed Left-handed Whelk only to examine more closely and see that I'd been fooled again; it was another Pear Whelk. I've never found one in all the years I've looked.

The Glacial Buccinum (*Buccinum glaciale Linné*) and Silky Buccinum (*Buccinum tenue Gray*) are found from the Arctic, down both sides of Canada to the United States.

A shell called Kellet's Whelk (*Kelletia kelleti Forbes*) is found from Santa Barbara south in California and Mexico.

In the rest of the world, northern Japan and southern New Zealand have cold-water species toward opposite poles. The Dilated Whelk (*Penion dilatatus Quoy* and *Gaimard*) gets to be as long as six inches, with a few longer specimens.

There are, of course, more tropical whelks, too. The Signum Whelk (*Siphonalia signum Reeve*) is common in Japan and decimates the oyster beds there. The Spiral Babylon (*Babylonia spirata Linné*) has Junonia spots and comes from Southeast Asia. There are others.

Closely allied to the whelks are the melongenas, the tulips, and the spindle shells. One of these is our King's Crown Conch (*Melongena corona Gmelin*), which is usually listed with the melongenas and not with the conchs, and which I've spoken of earlier. And another is the largest of all univalves, the Australian Trumpet (*Syrinx aruanus Linné*). This is a tremendous shell, sometimes just over two feet in length, and very impressive. As its name implies, trumpets have been made from it clear back to primitive times. Like any shell which is in some way tops, it is a conversation piece and a great help in putting together a collection that will be interesting to a viewer.

Only three or four inches behind it is the Florida Horse

49. Left-handed Whelk (*Busycon contrarium Conrad*), from which body, left, was removed intact.

50. Signum Whelk (*Siphonalia signum Reeve*); left and right, Hawk Wing Conchs (*Strombus raninus Gmelin*).

51. True Tulip (*Fasciolaria tulipa Linné*)

Conch (*Pleuroploca gigantea Kiener*), which I've already discussed. It, and the tulips, are very common along Gulf of Mexico beaches. There is the True Tulip (*Fasciolaria tulipa Linné*) and the Banded Tulip (*Fasciolaria hunteria Perry*). A dark red-colored tulip is semi-rare and much sought after on Florida beaches.

As for the Spindle Shells, these look like the Horse Conch, but have a longer siphonal canal. Their shape is extremely graceful, and even though they come from the Indo-Pacific area, they are often displayed in North America.

We've mentioned the abalone shells which you can find on the Pacific Coast, but we didn't mention that there are also abalone shells available in other areas of the world. Japan is a great producer; they are fished there commercially. South Africa, Australia, New Zealand, the western Pacific also have various species.

Mostly the United States West Coast varieties are named for colors. In order of size, they are the Red Abalone (*Haliotis rufescens Swainson*), the Green (*Haliotis fulgens Philippi*), the Pink (*Haliotis corrugata Gray*), the Black (*Haliotis cracherodi Leach*), the Northern Green (*Haliotis walallensis Stearns*).

The cheapest that I know of is the Japanese Abalone, (*Haliotis japonica Reeve*), a two-inch shell which sells as low as ten cents. And a four-inch Japanese variety, the Disc Abalone (*Haliotis discus Reeve*), is only a few cents more. Japan's Giant Abalone (*Haliotis gigantea Gmelin*) can be bought as low as half a dollar, lower than about half our own abalone shells.

The most interesting shape is the Donkey's Ear Abalone (*Haliotis asinina Linné*), which is shaped just as its name implies it should be and is from the western Pacific area. The fanciest seems to me to be the Australian shell, Three-ribbed Abalone (*Haliotis scalaris Leach*). The most interesting name is the More Beautiful Abalone (*Haliotis pulcherrima Gmelin*) from Polynesia.

Usually the eastern area of the United States, especially

52. Banded Tulips (*Fasciolaria hunteria* Perry)

53. Black Abalone (*Haliotis cracherodi* Leach)

Florida, is endowed with shell species more abundantly than the West Coast. But when it comes to abalones, Florida is an also-ran. There's just one: Pourtales' Abalone (*Haliotis pourtalesi Dall*). It is uncommon and is very small. So you Easterners, if you want abalone shells, you'll have to look far from home.

You know the story of the counterfeit wentletraps, but there are a number of wentletraps available to the shell collector along both North American coasts. The word "wentletrap" is from the Dutch, meaning winding staircase. These shells have a series of raised vertical ribs running from whorl to whorl from the apex to the mouth. They are very beautiful and delicately shaped shells. Most of them are comparatively small.

In eastern United States waters are Humphrey's Wentletrap (*Epitonium humphreysi Kiener*), the Angulate Wentletrap (*Epitonium angalatum Say*), the Brown-banded Wentletrap (*Epitonium rupicola Kurtz*), and the Lamellose Wentletrap (*Epitonium lamellosum Lamarck*). Those found in beach shelling are so small that a person without 20-20 vision should sit down to examine the shell piles for them. The lighthouse beach area on Sanibel Island is productive.

On the West Coast of the United States there are several. The Indian—or Money—(*Epitonium indianorum Carpenter*), the Tinted (*Epitonium tinctum Carpenter*) and the Greenland (*Epitonium groenlandicum Perry*) are the three which have the most pronounced vertical rib feature. These ribs, incidentally, come from a thickening of the lip of the shell between periods of shell-building. When the animal starts again, the thick edge is left and remains there as a rib.

In the rest of the world there are many of these shells, but Europe furnishes us the most common one, and it actually has that for its name: the Common Wentletrap (*Epitonium communis Linné*).

The helmet and bonnet shells are spectacular shells, attention-getters in any collection. The Caribbean area has a seven-inch King Helmet (*Cassis tuberosa Linné*) from which

54. Wentletraps (*Epitonium lamellosum Lamarck*)

shell cameos are sometimes cut. And an even larger one comes from the Indo-Pacific area and is called the Horned Helmet (*Cassis cornuta Linné*). This one runs just under a foot in length. These shells have cowrielike teeth in the

55. Bull-Mouth Helmet (*Cypraecassis rufa Linné*)

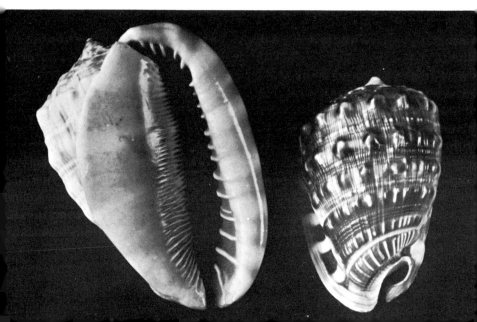

mouth. There are several which carry this cowrielike aperture. It is enough like a cowrie so that in Latin the cowrie name is added to the helmet name. Thus the Reticulated Cowrie-Helmet is called *Cypraecassis* (*Cypraecassis testiculus Linné*). It is from the Caribbean. The biggest of these shells is the Bull Mouth Helmet (*Cypraecassis rufa Linné*), which comes from the Indian Ocean and is another used in the manufacture of cameos.

The bonnets are smaller. The two best-known to United States collectors are the Scotch Bonnet (*Phalium granulatum Born*) and the Smooth Scotch Bonnet (*Phalium cicatricosum Gmelin*), both of which are far from common on Florida beaches, and much sought after by beach collectors. But North Carolina shell collectors call their state "the Scotch Bonnet State." The smooth variety comes from far enough south in the Caribbean so that it is seldom collected on the mainland.

There is also a very common shell in the Caribbean area called the Atlantic Woodlouse (*Morum oniscus Linné*), not a very appetizing title, which is another of this variety. It can, however, be found on Florida beaches.

The Indo-Pacfic area has the Channeled Bonnet (*Phalium canaliculata Bruguiere*), the Areola Bonnet (*Phalium areola Linné*), the Striped Bonnet (*Phalium strigatum Gmelin*), and the Gray Bonnet (*Phalium glaucum Linné*), all of which have the bonnet shape and are beautifully marked. Nowadays one is about as uncommon as the other.

We've told about the limpets called Coolie Hats, and these too are obtainable in various shapes and sizes in other parts of the world. The fanciest is the Maximum Keyhole Limpet (*Fissurella maxima Sowerby*) from Chile.

There is, too, the Mandarin's Hat, one of the top shells. There are a lot of these, all roughly the same shape; they are found the length of both our coasts. Ours are mostly in the inch-or-less class. But in New Zealand they have several gorgeous top shells as much as three inches long. And in Japan the Pyramid Top Shell (*Tectus pyramis Born*), with

56. Scotch Bonnets (*Phalium granulatum* Born)

a greenish tinge, is almost five inches long. Others there range up to that.

To add to the rest of the headgear-named shells—the helmets, bonnets, Coolie Hats, Mandarin's Hats—there are the turbans. There are some 500 varieties of these throughout the world, but the one we know well is the Chestnut Turban (*Turbo castanea* Gmelin), which is found on our Florida coast and farther south. The Green Turban from Australia (*Turbo marmoratus* Linné) is the largest at about eight and a half inches and has a bigger mouth even than some of our prizefighters.

Along with the rest of the headgear, too, there are the miters, a large family—some 625 types in all. They are shaped

57. Striped Bonnets (*Phalium strigatum* Gmelin)

a little like the United States volutes, and have a very long snout.

Naturally the names have to do with the church. There is the Episcopal Miter (*Mitra mitra Linné*), the Pontifical Miter (*Mitra stictica Link*), the Papal Miter (*Mitra papalis Linné*), and the Imperial Miter (*Mitra imperialis Röding*). I hasten to add, however, that the Blood-sucker Miter (*Mitra sanguisuga Linné*) was definitely *not* named as these others were. Most come from the Indo-Pacific area, but we do have two that are common in the Caribbean. They are the Barbados Miter (*Mitra barbedensis Gmelin*) and the Nodulose Miter (*Mitra nodulosa Gmelin*).

I have told you about the use of shells as trumpets in religious ceremonies, in war, even in calling hotel guests to dinner. The triton trumpets lend themselves to this use along with the ones I have mentioned, which are the huge melongena called the Australian Trumpet and our Horse Conch. The Pacific Triton (*Charonia tritonis Linné*) and the Atlantic Trumpet (*Charonia variegata Lamarck*) and the Knobbed Triton (*Charonia nodifera Lamarck*) from the Mediterranean are beautifully marked and imposing in size. They range up to sixteen inches and should be, if possible, in all collections. Smaller are the Hairy Tritons, which have a periostracum which looks a little like a pelt.

The augers are easily collected. Along the Atlantic Coast, especially from North Carolina south, a number of species can be had for the taking almost any time. The easiest to come by are in the inch class. Augers are a very long, narrow shell. They are narrow even at the base, and grow symmetrically narrower to the pointed apex; they look like a Canadian jack pine tree. The Atlantic Auger (*Terebra dislocata Say*), the Shiny Atlantic Auger (*Terebra hastata Gmelin*) and the Fine-ribbed Auger (*Terebra protexta Conrad*) are so common that they are worth about a penny each. In California there is the reasonably common San Pedro Auger (*Terebra pedroana Dall*).

For the showy members of this family, you have to go

mostly to foreign lands, though there is the Flame Auger in the Gulf of Mexico and the West Indies (*Terebra taurina Solander*), which reaches half a foot in length.

In the Indo-Pacific area, besides some smaller ones, there are the Dimidiate Auger (*Terebra dimidiata Linné*), the Muscaria Auger (*Terebra areolata Link*), the Subulate Auger (*Terebra subulata Linné*), all growing to about half a foot and all gorgeously marked. The biggest and showiest of all is the Pacific Marlinspike Auger (*Terebra maculata Linné*), which gets to be just under a foot in length.

For turret shells your best bet is a trade with some Japanese collector. Over there they have some 410 species. However, here we have a number of less spectacular species, mosly on the East Coast. The one that closest approaches the showy Japanese turrets is the Common Star Turret (*Ancistrosyrinx radiata Dall*), which is usually obtained by dredging. The one with the most amusing name is the Delicate Giant Turret (*Polystira tellea Dall*). On the Pacific Coast there are two, the Filose Turret and the Beaded Turret (*Mitromorpha filosa Carpenter* and *Mitromorpha aspera Carpenter*).

Of the Japanese turrets, by far the most unusual is the Miraculous Thatcheria (*Thatcheria mirabilis Sowerby*), which looks a little like a wide road built up a steep cone-shaped mountain to the castle on top.

The Cat's Eye and the Tiger's Eye are moon shells. These are fairly easy to find from Canada south. In the Indo-Pacific area, though, there are a number of species which are even more spectacular than ours. The China Moon (*Natica onca Röding*) and the Zebra Moon (*Natica zebra Lamarck*) are two of these. When scientists were faced with stripes, obviously "zebra" was the first thing that came to mind.

The frog shells are tropical enough so that you'll probably have to trade for them. The one to look for, the big one, is the Giant Frog (*Bursa bubo Linné*), which isn't too hard to acquire, and is in the ten-inch category.

Among the star shells, the Caribbean has the Long-spined

58. Cat's Eyes or Shark Eyes (*Polinices duplicatus Say*)

Star (*Astraea phoebia Röding*). The Bleeding Tooth mentioned in Chapter 2 is one of the nerites. Another from roughly the same area is the tiny Emerald Nerite (*Smaragdia viridis Linné*), and there are others from other parts of the globe.

We have in the United States the Common European Periwinkle (*Littorina littorea Linné*), which has worked its way south as far as Virginia in the last several hundred years. And the tun and fig shells are both available to us in the United States. The Giant Tun (*Tonna galea Linné*) is available in almost all tropical waters of the world. And the Grinning Tun (*Malea ringens Swainson*) is found on the Pacific coast of Central America. The Caribbean Tun (*Tonna maculosa Dillwyn*), sometimes called Partridge Tun, is found from Florida to Central America.

The Atlantic Fig (*Ficus communis Röding*) is common on southeastern beaches. It's a fragile shell, and hard to beach-collect in perfect condition. For some reason there's one spot just west of the Island Inn on Sanibel where I can almost always pick up figs.

There are rock shells to be collected. The easiest for Americans is the Wide-mouthed Purpura (*Purpura patula Linné*), a shell that looks like Martha Raye singing. I've mentioned

59. Common Fig Shells (*Ficus communis Röding*)

60. Harp Shell (*Harpa costata Linné*)

61. Nutmegs (*Cancellaria reticulata Linné*)

the local Carrier Shell, the shell-collector among shells, (*Xenophora conchyliophora Born*). The Japanese have one, *Xenophora pallidula Reeve*, which is bigger, and the American Pacific area has the Sunburst Carrier (*Stellaria solaris Linné*), which is about halfway between the other two in size.

The harp shells are a bit like the tuns, but have ridges that look like the strings of a harp. Probably these ridges, just as in the wentletraps, represent a thickening of the lip between periods of growth.

Bubbles, nutmegs, margin shells, oyster drills are easy to collect. And there are many others; of necessity we've only hit the high spots.

We find, then, that the shells divide into families and some families are very large indeed. Each presents a challenge to the collector to acquire as many of its members as he can. There are thousands upon thousands in all; no person can collect them all, but it's fun to try.

13

Everyday Shells—Bivalves

YOU will find that collecting bivalves is much different from collecting univalves. Among univalves, the difference between two cowries or cones, for instance, is for the most part a considerable difference in shape. The difference between the various clams or the various cockles, on the other hand, is much less a difference of basic shape and more a difference of markings, hinges, position of beak, lines, ridges, thickness of shell. You have a tendency to think of each cone separately. But a pecten—any pecten—is just a scallop, and none but the expert conchologist thinks of it as a Calico Scallop, a Rough Scallop, a Mildred's Scallop, or an Ornate Scallop. These are all so much alike that the differences make no impression on the layman.

You can, therefore, have a fantastically large collection of bivalves with no duplicates, yet the person you show it to will be unimpressed and think of it as mostly duplicates and triplicates and quadruplicates.

In this chapter, therefore, we will tell you how to be represented easiest in each family, but we won't touch much on the more minute deviations. Once you have the major types, you can build on them as much or as little as you like.

Another difference between univalves and bivalves: the eastern part of the United States has all the best of the univalves, but the Pacific Coast is its equal, perhaps even its superior in the case of the bivalves.

And, though obviously there are clams and oysters everywhere, nobody is going to bother much in this country about a European oyster shell or clam shell unless it is extremely different or ornate. There won't, therefore, be anywhere near as many foreign bivalves as foreign univalves in most collections.

Many bivalves are so plentiful that they are useless for collection purposes except to have one representative specimen. Finally, there are nowhere near the number or percentage of rare bivalves; nothing to compare with the Glory-of-the-Seas Cone or the Prince Cowrie.

To me the pectens or scallops are the most interesting of the bivalves. Certainly they are as colorful as any.

The two that you are most likely to come in contact with gastronomically are the Atlantic Deep-sea Scallop (*Placopecten magellanicus Gmelin*) and the Atlantic Bay Scallop (*Aequipecten irradians Lamarck*). The Deep-sea has the smoother, rounder shell. The Bay has the more typical pecten shape and has radiating ribs. Both are fished extensively for food; in both the adductor muscle is delicious.

The Calico Scallop (*Aequipecten gibbus Linné*), found along the west coast of Florida, is the most colorful. When scallops are "in" on the beach it is almost impossible to leave them alone, they are so beautiful. Just when you decide you have all you can carry, a particularly lovely combination of purples with a fleck of yellow will tempt you too much. The color combinations are almost limitless. There are many, many other scallops from Labrador south.

On the Pacific Coast there is the Giant Pacific Scallop (*Pecten diegensis Dall*), which is fished commercially in northern areas and corresponds to the two commercial varieties of the East Coast. There are also the beautiful Pacific Pink Scallop (*Chlamys hastata hericia Gould*) and Hind's Scallop (*Chlamys hindsi Dall*) and many others. The most amazing is the Giant Rock Scallop (*Hinnites multirugosus Gale*), which has been known to weigh nineteen pounds.

Besides the scallops, which have both valves convex, there

are a number of kinds which have the lower valve deep and convex, and the upper valve flat and colorful. This upper valve, is called a fan. The Zigzag Scallop (*Pecten ziczac Linné*) is a classic example. These fans are a conversation piece, and even though they are medium rare, are obtainable by a conscientious collector.

There are huge fans from Japan. There are, too, the Noble Scallop and Swift's Scallop (*Chlamys nobilis Reeve* and *Chlamys swifti Bernardi*) from the same area. Farther south, in Asian waters, there is the round Asian Moon Scallop (*Amusium pleuronectes Linné*). And even the little Cat's Paw (*Plicatula gibbosa Lamarck*), which is such an interesting shell for children in our own area, is a form of pecten. In fact interesting, colorful scallops abound just about everywhere—from North Carolina south through the Gulf States and the West Indies.

The clams are a huge family and just about as colorless as the scallops are colorful. We have already described the largest of them all, the Giant Clam (*Tridacna gigas Linné*).

It is difficult to advise collectors what they should do about clams. For instance the Northern Quahog (*Mercenaria mercenaria Linné*) and the Southern Quahog (*Mercenaria campechiensis Gmelin*) are so common and used so often for chowder and even clams on the half shell—especially the Northern—that no other shell anywhere would be easier to collect. These, when young, are called "littleneck," and the Pacific Coast has the Thin-shelled Littleneck (*Protothaca tenerrima Carpenter*), the Common Pacific Littleneck (*Protothaca staminea Conrad*), and the very common and edible Common Washington Clam (*Saxidomus nuttalli Conrad*). You will see the shells of all these clams used in shore areas as ashtrays, pin dishes, and in dozens of other ways. It would seem a little silly to have one in a collection. Yet it was from the Northern Quahog that wampum was manufactured by the eastern Indians. Because of that, possibly that one is needed.

Experts do not agree about whether or not the Quahog is

one of the huge designation of Venus clams. There are literally hundreds of these. Several are more colorful than most clams, and still very easy to acquire. One of these is the Sunray Venus (*Macrocallista nimbosa Solander*). This is plentiful along beaches of the southeastern United States and is one of the few very showy shells among the clams. Another is the Calico Clam (*Macrocallista maculata Linné*), which has brown checkerboard markings and is quite striking. In California there is the Pismo Clam (*Tivela stultorum Mawe*), which also has interesting radiating markings.

There are many, many other easy-to-collect Venus clams on both coasts. There is one somewhat uncommon variety which is worth mentioning: the Royal Comb Venus (*Pitar dione Linné*). This is in no way to be confused with the univalve, the Venus Comb, even though it does have long spines. These spines are what lend the shell its interest. They are roughly as long as the shell is high. They are based in

63. Sunray (*Macrocallista nimbosa Solander*) surrounded by Sunrise Tellins (*Tellina radiata Linné*)

64. Rose Petal Tellins (*Tellina lineata Turton*)

the raised growth rings and have a superficial look of comb teeth. They make the single valve of the shell look like a woman's hat with long, rounded feather ornaments at a rakish angle. The shell is washed up on the beaches from Texas down the Mexican coast. A Pacific Coast variety (*Pitar lupanaria Lesson*) occurs from Lower California south. As I've said, these Venus clams occur all over the world. The Lettered Venus from the Indo-Pacific area (*Tapes literata Linné*) is a very beautiful shell. The Cross-barred Venus (*Chione cancellata Linné*) is a very common shell, and not only has the regular clam growth ridges but has vertical ridges, too, making a pattern of tiny squares. The Common Californian Venus is not a movie actress, but rather the name of a very usual Pacific Coast shell (*Chione californiensis Broderip*). The Wedding Cake Venus (*Callanaitis disjecta Perry*) has the most interesting name.

The tellins are the most beautiful of the clams, in my opinion. You can easily find the fragile Sunrise Tellin (*Tellina radiata Linné*) along Florida beaches. Even more beautiful is the Candy Stick Tellin (*Tellina similis Sowerby*). And it is no trick at all to collect the Rose Petal Tellin (*Tellina lineata Turton*), along the beaches of the protected waters of the west coast of Florida. There are many, many other tellins on both coasts, but these are the easiest ones.

There are the awning clams, which get their name from the fact that their periostracum sticks out past the edges of the valves and so looks like an awning. They are present on both coasts. And there are the nut clams, also present on both coasts. There are a lot of them, and the difference between them is not great.

It is easy, too, to find many, many kinds of mussels on both coasts and collect far more than you can ever use. They live in dense clusters on rocks and pilings. Many animals eat them, including man. The Blue Edible Mussel (*Mytilus edulis Linné*) is most famous rock-dwelling variety. It is found along both coasts from the Arctic regions south. It has a bluish tinge. The Atlantic Ribbed Mussel (*Modiolus*

65. Buttercups (*Anodontia alba Link*)

demissus Rafinesque) is also common and found on both coasts in swamp moss.

Someone has even added to the amazing numbers and variations of mussels a False Mussel. And in addition to all the regular clams, there is a Coral-boring Clam (*Coralliophaga coralliophaga Gmelin*) and both an Atlantic and a Pacific Cleft Clam (*Thyasira trisinuata Orbigny* and *Thyasira bisecta Conrad*), which look like any ordinary clam except for the cleft from the apex to the lip.

There are a whole lot of lucinas (more than 200 of them) which look like each other and like clams; maybe a little fancier than some, but clams just the same. The easiest of these to collect is the Buttercup (*Anodontia alba Link*), which has a butter-colored interior.

And there are the file clams, which can swim. There are many of these all over the world. The Spiny Lima (*Lima lima Linné*) and the Rough Lima (*Lima scabra Born*) are two of the better known. The Rough Lima, alive, has a mat of reddish tentacles, some more than half as long as the shell itself, which line the opening from one hinge end around to the other. It looks like a clam that has just chomped onto a mouthful of red spaghetti, and this, along with its swimming capabilities, makes it a very interesting species.

I can't overemphasize two things: that these bivalves are

for the most part common, and that the differences between them are minute for the layman and the beginner, even though they are very real. There are gem clams, dosinia clams, rupellaria clams, and a whole lot of semeles and macomas. There are abras and cumingias. There are the tagelus clams and the donax (and even false donax) clams.

We have already talked about one very very common donax, the Coquina (*Donax variabilis Say*), and we will talk about the gathering of these for broth in detail later.

There are a lot of different surf clams and duck clams on both coasts. At least one, Stimpson's Surf Clam (*Spisula polynyma Stimpson*), is found in northern areas on both coasts and even over in Japan. The Atlantic Surf Clam (*Spisula solidissima Dillwyn*) is another of those that are in such vast supply that to put one in a collection seems a bit absurd. Thousands upon thousands of them wash up on eastern beaches after winter storms. This is the clam from which commercial canned chowder is most often made. Hians Surf Clam from Asia (*Mactra hians Philippi*) has Coquinalike markings.

One of the easiest duck clams to collect is the Channeled Duck Clam, which I call a Sailor's Ear (*Labiosa plicatella Lamarck*). Some winters I have seen stretches of beach that were covered by these delicate shells. They look as if they couldn't stand anything, yet are often found on the beach whole, even double.

There is, believe it or not, a Propeller Clam (*Cyrtodaria siliqua Spengler*), which gets its name from the twisted propeller-blade shape of the shell.

And the mya clams have a member which is as ridiculously plentiful as the Atlantic Surf Clam. This is the Soft-Shell Clam (*Mya arenaria Linné*), and on the Pacific coast the (*Mya japonica Jay*) produces over a million dollars' worth of gourmet food a year. The leptons, a parasite clam, sound like a brand of tea, but aren't.

There are the corbulas and the Geoduck or Gooeyduck (*Panope generosa Gould*), and the lovely Angel Wing

(*Barnea costata Linné*), mentioned earlier. To confuse the issue and you, there are the False Angel Wing (*Petricola pholadiformis Lamarck*), which has the regular Angel Wing ridges only part way along its larger end, and the Fallen Angel Wing (*Barnea truncata Say*), which is fairly common.

There are piddocks on both coasts, and the bivalves that bore into things that I've told you about. There are several species which bore into old shells, one into abalone shells. But the ones that are famous for the damage they do are the shipworms with their small scraping valves at one end (*Teredo navalis Linné*).

There are others, the spoon clams and the cuspidarias among them. There is one pandora which looks as if somebody had cut an ordinary clam shell in half lengthwise. This is Say's Pandora (*Pandora trilineata Say*).

We have spoken before, too, about the jackknife and razor clams which look like the handle of an old-fashioned straight razor. The animals in some of these are fine eating. The Atlantic Razor Clam (*Siliqua costata Say*) and the Pacific Razor Clam (*Siliqua patula Dixon*) are very easy to collect.

So you can see that among the clams, the possibilities for the collector are almost limitless, though admittedly the challenge is not great.

As a transition between the clams and the oysters, I'll mention again the gorgeous Thorny Oysters, though they are nothing like the true oysters. These large, showy, highly colored shells with their long spines, which have such a flowerlike appearance, are like the pectens in making you forget the differences between them and concentrate on their colors and their beauty. The Pacific Thorny Oyster (*Spondylus pictorum Schreiber*) is more colorful even than the Atlantic variety (*Spondylus americanus Hermann*). The Regal Thorny Oyster (*Spondylus regius Linné*) from Southeast Asian waters is spectacular and grows to be as much as nine inches in length. Remember the spectacular exhibit of these in the Florida Marine Museum at Fort Myers, Florida.

The Leafy Jewel Box (*Chama macerophylla Gmelin*) grows spines long enough so that it is sometimes taken for a Spiny Oyster. Other jewel boxes are found attached to pen shells and other objects and are a bit hard to come by with both valves and hinge perfect. One valve is simple enough, but nobody wants a box with only a cover. The Little Corrugated Jewel Box (*Chama congregata Conrad*) is the one to try for from North Carolina south.

The jingle shells attach themselves to pen and ark shells, as do the jewel boxes, and to each other. If you bring up something on which a lot of these, alive, are attached to one another with their shells open, you can touch the top one and cause it to close. This movement will be telegraphed in order to those below and in turn they will clamp together. They look like isinglass, have one valve with a hole in it, and if you pick up a number of empty jingles and shake them, they really do jingle. The easiest to find is the Common Jingle Shell (*Anomia simplex Orbigny*), and the Pacific area has a large False Jingle Shell (*Pododesmus macroschismus Deshayes*), which grows to be three or four inches in diameter. Along the Gulf of Mexico you often find black jingles, and this is not necessarily the way they started out in life. If jingles are a long time buried in muddy sand or plain mud, they turn black.

True oysters are plentiful all over the world. And this shell probably leads the parade of what-of-it shells from a collector's point of view. All you have to do to get a pair of shells for your collection is to go to the back door of your favorite seafood restaurant.

The Native Pacific Oyster (*Ostrea lurida Carpenter*) and the Chesapeake Bay—sometimes called Eastern—Oyster (*Crassostrea virginica Gmelin*) are the backbone of a huge industry which we will talk more about in a later chapter. There are many other types of oysters, and these have been complicated by the fact that the Giant Pacific Oyster (*Crassostrea gigas Thunberg*) has been introduced into Canada and the United States from Japan because of its size, and

66. Leafy Jewel Box (*Chama macerophylla* Conrad)

the Chesapeake Oyster has been tried in a lot of places. It has been tested even in Europe, which has some pretty fine oysters of its own. One type that I find delicious is the Mangrove Oyster (*Ostrea frons Linné*)—sometimes called 'Coon Oyster—which I've already explained literally grows on trees: mangrove trees, that is.

We have the Atlantic Pearl Oyster (*Pinctada radiata*

67. Jingle Shells (*Anomia simplex* Orbigny)

68. Atlantic Wing Oysters (*Pteria colymbus Röding*)

Leach). In other parts of the world pearl oysters are famous. There are half a dozen species which produce a nacre so lustrous that when they cover foreign bodies in the shell, as I've shown you, the resulting pearl is marketable. The Black-lipped (*Pinctada margaritifera Linné*) of Southeast Asia and the Japanese Oyster (*Pinctada mertensi Dunker*) are very well known.

The wing and hammer oysters are extremely interesting in their shape. We have the Atlantic Wing Oyster (*Pteria colymbus Röding*). These have on one side an elongation of the "wings" of the hinge. The pectens have these wings sometimes, longer on one side than the other. But in the Atlantic Wing Oyster, the long thin wing extends out so far that it almost doubles the width of the shell. These are found on beaches from North Carolina south. On the Pacific Coast there is the Western Wing Oyster (*Pteria sterna Gould*), which is even larger. And in the Indo-Pacific area, there is the Giant Wing Oyster (*Pteria penguin Röding*), which grows as long as six and a half inches.

The Hammer Oysters are found in the Indo-Pacific and

have the extension of the hinge of the Atlantic Wing, but have it on both sides of the hinge (but not the same length each side) and have such a long body that the whole is a dead ringer for a pickaxe. The Common Hammer Oyster (*Malleus malleus Linné*) is another conversation piece. The White Hammer Oyster (*Malleus albus Lamarck*) is about as common and even more of an "oh-my" shell because it is white.

I've introduced the Turkey Wing and mentioned that it is an ark shell. There are an infinite number of these ark shells and you can pick up doubles of several kinds anytime you walk out onto a southern beach.

Pen shells are far, far too plentiful in many places after storms. They are a large, thin, brittle brown shell which looks like the instrument which our great-grandfathers used to hold the sand with which they blotted their writings. The shell is pointed at one end, about four inches wide at the other. The material is iridescent and pieces of it have lovely purple tinges. The American Pen Shell (*Atrina rigida Solander*) is so large that when it is washed up in quantity on a beach (see picture, page 99) the beach takes on an incredibly littered look and hotel and cottage owners have to rake these shells away so that they can use the beach. This is the shell whose byssus threads were used to weave into expensive items of clothing.

There remain then the cockles. Here again we have a very plentiful species. The shells are deep, medium thick. The animal inside is therefore large in comparison to the size of the shell. And you can imagine what a feast one of these bivalves about four inches in diameter is for a lucky univalve that can make the conquest. Or a gull that finds one, flies high with it, and drops it to break it open.

The cockle itself is famous in song and story. Remember "crying cockles and mussels, alive, alive-o"? The shells are used in making shell articles, and as cooking dishes, ashtrays, family change holders and as receptacles for many other things. My wife cooks a scalloped fish or crab concoction in cockle shells and then brings the food to the table right in the shell, one shell to each individual.

These shells are so plentiful on Sanibel Island after a storm that you can pick the size you want to serve in, giant for main course and big eaters, smaller for second helpings. And even smaller if you're going to use the material for hors d'oeuvres.

The big one is the Giant Atlantic Cockle (*Dinocardium robustum Solander*), and it is robust, all right. The one we personally cook in, as I've mentioned above, is a subgenus called Vanhyning's Cockle (*Dinocardium rubustum vanhyningi Clench and L. C. Smith*). It's a little more colorful than the Giant Atlantic.

The West Coast has a number of cockles. The Giant Pacific Cockle, which is called Spiny Cockle (*Trachycardium quadragenarium Conrad*) in some areas, is fairly common. The area also has an Egg Cockle, a small one, called the Common Pacific Egg Cockle (*Laevicardium substriatum Conrad*).

The Plover's Egg (*Laevicardium laevigatum Linné*) is easy to collect on Florida beaches, and is a nicely shaped shell. The small Yellow Cockle (*Trachycardium muricatum Linné*) with its bright yellow color is extremely common. Morton's Cockle (*Laevicardium mortoni Conrad*) is plentiful everywhere along the Eastern Seaboard, but this small cockle is a favorite with the bird life of Cape Cod as a staple food.

There are, as the song we quoted implies, beautiful cockles in England, European countries, and of course in the Indo-Pacific area. The European Cockle (*Cerastoderma edule Linné*) is a food staple, and its brown shell is nicely ribbed and marked. In the Indo-Pacific there is a cockle with a perfect heart shape when both valves are viewed from the side. It is called the Heart Cockle (*Corculum cardissa Linné*) and it is a fairly common shell which shouldn't be hard to acquire. Once acquired it is admired by all who see it. You would have to go to more than half the trouble of getting the Heart if you wanted to acquire the Half-Heart Cockle

69. Common Egg Cockle (*Laevicardium laevigatum* Linné)

70. Left to right, Glycymerius shell (*Glycymerius latiocostata*), Atlantic Bay Scallop (*Aequipecten irradians* Lamarck), Hinnites Scallop (*Hinnites multirugosus* Gale)

(*Hemicardium hemicardium Linné*). This purple-tinged, lovely shell is fairly hard to come by.

So, there are some of the interesting shells for collectors of bivalves. And in this field you can make a much fuller showing, at no expense at all, than can ever be done with univalves, because members of almost every group are so plentiful. You can get a lot more show for less expense of time and money, but what you get in that way will be far less solid.

Many of these are beautiful, especially the pectens, the tellins and also the thorny Chrysanthemum Shells described in Chapter 11. Any collection that contains many representations in these fields cannot help being spectacular.

14

Rare, Freak, Unusual Shells

S UPPLY and demand, with minor exceptions, rules in setting shell values, just as it does in so many other fields. And
the values often change rapidly; something that was very
rare goes from a high price to a low after an abundant supply has been discovered. A perfect example of this is the
Junonia. When I did an article on the islands off the west
coast of Florida many years ago, in my research I found
some mention of a Junonia worth $2,000. By the time I
began to spend winters at Sanibel Island, the Junonia offered there in the winter Shell Fair raffle was advertised as
being worth $175. The shrimp boats had by then begun to
bring up perfect specimens in their nets and had put them
on the market; the price kept dropping until now it is about
$10 for a really long, perfect Junonia and $5 for a run-of-
the-mill shell.

Which brings us to a second interesting fact. The shell is
still just as hard to find on the beach as it ever was; it was
just the shell-shop supply which increased. As far as I can
see, these two facts are kept completely separate by the shell
collectors there. Finding a Junonia on an early-morning expedition is just as much a triumph as it ever was. It is still
the ultimate, the end of the rainbow for beach collectors. It
still furnishes rewards immeasurable in money.

So you have two types of supply and demand. The actual
Junonia supply has risen till it approaches the demands of

buyers. But the collectable supply has not increased and the collectors' demands for Junonias for beach pick-up has not decreased.

The Cedo-nulli Cone (*Conus cedo-nulli*) is an older and far more famous example. This brought fantastic prices at sales in the 1700s and 1800s. It was a very famous and valuable shell. It is still called the Cedo-nulli Cone, but it goes under a different title now (*Conus dominicanus Hwass*) and would now sell for less than five inflated dollars. In the same way the Royal Comb Venus (*Pitar dione Linné*), that interesting bivalve with the spikes, was at one time so rare that Rumphius, who was one of the very earliest of shell collectors, offered $5000 for a perfect specimen. And that was in old-fashioned dollars. Today these shells aren't exactly a dime a dozen, but neither by any stretch of the imagination could they be called a rare shell.

You already know that I look upon the Glory-of-the-Seas Cone as the world's most valuable shell. It probably isn't the rarest; Roderick Cameron claims in his book, *Shells*, that there are only two known specimens of the Leucodon Cowrie (*Cypraea leucodon Broderip*), one of which is owned by the British Museum and the other by the Harvard University Museum. He also says there are only nine known specimens of the Clytospira Cone (*Conus clytospira Melvill and Standen*). But somehow the Glory-of-the-Seas has captured the imagination of the shell-gathering world. Possibly its name contributes. After all, the name Glory-of-the-Seas would fire your interest far more than, say, the Clytospira Cone. The one opens all sorts of mental vistas, the other is, the first time you meet it, just an exercise in pronunciation.

Whatever the reason, the Glory-of-the-Seas is world-famous and has been for centuries. There are all sorts of stories circulated about it, some of them probably true. One which may or may not be true is that three specimens were found on a reef by Hugh Cuming in 1838. And when he went back for more, the reef was gone because of earthquake action; no more Glory-of-the-Seas, ever. Other specimens have

71. Miss Mugridge's Glory-of-the Sea Cone (*Conus gloria-maris Chemnitz*) in the holder she devised.

Good shelling Ede Mugridge Sanibel Island Jan. 29/68

72. Copy of the letter which the Australian bank sent to Miss Mugridge.

COMMONWEALTH TRADING BANK OF AUSTRALIA
KAVIENG, T.P.N.G.

CABLE "CONTRABANK"
TELEPHONE: 68

REPLY: THE MANAGER,
BOX 45, P.O. KAVIENG, T.P.N.G.
REFERENCE:

30/4/65.

Miss E.H.Mugridge,
Gulf Drive,
Sanibel Island,
FLORIDA.

Dear Miss Mugridge,

      Mr. Neale of our Rabaul Branch has sent me your letter of the 2rd.April for reply as this branch has been dealing with the finder of the shell.

      The finder,Matai,a New Guinean, was spear fishing at night with flares on a coral reef when he saw the shell in about 6 feet of water and dived for it.He was fishing on the surface of the water not beneath. He was about 100 yards from the shore near Sumuna Village on the island of Djaul about 20 miles from New Ireland. There are no small maps of the immediate area but we are enclosing a sketch plan of the area so that you can orientate the position on a larger map which you probably have.

      A receipt for the amount from the finder is enclosed. As a matter of interest the money has been credited to an account at this bank and the native concerned intends to set up a small store on his island to sell goods to his fellow villagers.

Yours sincerely,

G.R.Waterson,
Manager.

since been found, therefore at least the conclusion was false even if the story itself is true.

And in the Glory's earliest history when only two specimens were known, the owner of one, who had thought it was the only one, bid outrageously for the second. When he got it he crashed it against the stone floor and broke it, triumphantly informing the world that now his *was* the only one. There has been at least one novel titled *The Glory of the Sea*; its plot hinged upon the theft of one of these shells.

One story the truth of which I *can* guarantee, because I have examined the papers, has to do with the finding of the specimen which we have photographed for this book. This belongs to Miss Edith Mugridge, owner of the Glory of the Sea shell shop on Sanibel Island.

Miss Mugridge wanted to buy one on the theory that a shop of that name should have one to show. Through R. Tucker Abbot of the Museum of Natural History in Philadelphia, who in my opinion knows more about these matters than anybody else anywhere, she was put in touch with the representative of a native of Rabaul, which is on New Britain Island in the Bismarck Archipelago down near Australia.

The native had been spear fishing on the surface in about six feet of water. He looked down and saw the Glory-of-the-Seas and dove for it. Miss Mugridge purchased the shell and made her remittance through an Australian bank. You will find a photostatic copy of their letter of acknowledgment on page 186.

They say that with this money the native, Matai, will purchase a store on his native island and sell merchandise to his fellow townsmen. Thus he will go from hand-to-mouth spear fisherman to moneyed businessman on the strength of just one Glory-of-the-Seas Cone. So pleased is he with Miss Mugridge's fairness in price that he has promised to send all future shells he may find to her. And he has invited her to stay with his family if she ever comes to his Rabaul. She says, "Who knows, I might just do that sometime."

Most reference works say that there are "25 known specimens extant." But Miss Mugridge has been told that hers is Number 30. The specimen she obtained is perfect in every detail with no chip or any other blemish along the lip. Its color is outstanding. She has arranged a holder—the one shown in the photograph—which is connected to the second hand mechanism of a watch. This turns the shell very slowly around once each minute.

Most families of shells have a lot of common shells, with perhaps one or two which are rare. The slit shells are an exception. These beautiful creations are all very valuable. There aren't many living species; they have the generic name *Pleurotomaria*. They are, in alphabetical order, *adansoniana, africana, amabilis, beyrichii, hirasei* (Emperor's Slit Shell), *quoyana, rumphii, salmiana, teramachii*. Each of these is worth over $250, with the exception of *hirasei* at under $20. The *rumphii* and *teramachii* are more then $500. Such a record isn't even approached by any other family of shells. Incidentally, *herasei* was once fabulously valuable.

But the cowries have individual shells which could, in a money sense, make three of any of the slit shells. The Prince Cowrie, which is also called the Brindled Cowrie (*Cypraea valentia Perry*), tops the list. It is hard to set a figure because actual prices depend so much on how badly the buyer wants to buy. But a fine specimen of the Prince Cowrie would probably be worth between $1,500 and $2,000. Imagine turning over a rock in Australia or India to see nearly $2000 staring you in the face.

We mentioned the Leucodon Cowrie at the beginning of this chapter in connection with the number of known specimens. The Leucodon (*Cypraea leucodon Broderip*) might bring you around $1500. Here again, if you were a fine bargainer and the bargainee really wanted the shell badly, you might do much better than that.

In almost exactly the same money area is the Great Spotted

Cowrie from the islands of the southwest Pacific (*Cypraea guttata Gmelin*). The Zoological Museum of Amsterdam owns the world record in this shell.

Dropping down another $500 to $1,000 or so, there is Barclay's Cowrie (*Cypraea barclayi Reeve*).

There are a lot of other valuable cowries, but not that valuable. Perhaps the best known of the rest is the Golden Cowrie, sometimes also called the Orange Cowrie (*Cypraea aurantium Gmelin*), which catches the imagination because it is so full and so nearly round, and such a gorgeous color. It is breathtaking; the orange color looks like a big drop of blood. The value might run up to $200 for a fine specimen. But collectors enjoy owning and displaying the shell far in excess of that amount of money. Broderip's Cowrie (*Cypraea broderipi Sowerby*) would be worth about the same, possibly a little more, and so would Surinam's (*surinamensis*).

Teramachi's Cowrie (*Cypraea teramachii Kuroda*) might be worth double that. Teramachi seems to have had many really valuable shells named for him. You will remember Teramachi's was among the slit shells, also at near the $500 mark. There are quite a few each side of $100, and many many at more than $10. Next to the slit shells and the volutes, the cowries are the most valuable as a genus even though the specimens at less than a quarter far outnumber the expensive ones.

As we've told you, the volutes, being a deep-water species for the most part, have no pikers in their ranks. There is, as far as I know, only one nickel-and-dime volute and that's the Bat Volute which I talked about. There is scarcely even a handful of $1 volutes. The average must be somewhere between $10 and $20. They don't have any over-$500 specimens, but there are a fantastic number in the $15 to $100 class.

The Alabaster Volute (*alabastrina*) is the most valuable. The Festive Volute (*festiva*) and the Spartan Volute (*sparta*) are the next highest in price and none of them are over $500. Still, that's a lot of money.

We mentioned too, the Clytospira Cone in connection with Cameron's statement that only nine of these cones exist. This is the only *cone* besides the Glory-of-the-Seas which would bring $1,000 if the specimen were good enough. There are other valuable cones that you would be delighted to find and own, both from a financial and an aesthetic point of view. But those two are the top ones.

So here I've described a handful of the world's most valuable and rarest shells. Admittedly you and I aren't going to find these. It is more to the point, then, to look for the locally rare shells on any beach you visit. These you have a chance of collecting.

Each area has its rare ones, and local collectors know which they are and will tell you. I personally have more first-hand knowledge of the west coast of Florida than any other area and I will use that area as an example. For the shells which I mention, substitute the rare shells from the area you yourself visit and shell.

There's the Junonia, the tops in the area. And there is the Golden Olive, about as rare. And the Golden Cockle, a very beautiful shell. Cockles are a dime a dozen, and I mean that literally; the Golden Cockle is something else again, and you may go for years, even on Florida's finest west coast shell beach, and never find one.

You might hunt the Lion's Paw and the Scotch Bonnet for several years without finding one in an acceptable specimen. Single valves of the Lion's Paw are, of course, many times more common than both valves with intact hinge. It's possible to find a live Lion's Paw on the beach, but it isn't probable in an ordinary man's lifetime.

Not common, but a little more frequent than the shells above, are the fans, especially complete with the deep undervalve. And the Lemon Pecten (or pure yellow scallop). There are many others, but these are the rarest.

Circumstances, though, change values. And so far we have talked in this chapter about normal shells. Deviations from

the normal in shells, freak specimens, are something different. A whole new set of values arises.

For instance, a Junonia that would be worth $5 if it were
normal would be worth nearly $2,000 if it were left-handed.
As far as I know there is only one specimen of a left-handed
Junonia in the world. The West Indian Chank Shell, worth
a couple of dollars in its ordinary form, is worth between
$500 and $1,000 left-handed, or sinistral. We've told you
about the use these rare left-handed specimens are put to in
the temples. The Queen Conch, left-handed, would be
worth several hundred dollars while the normal shell would
be worth less than a dollar.

The same rule applies to a left-handed shell like the Left-
handed Whelk (*Busycon contrarium Conrad*) shown below.
In this case, though, the right-handed specimen in the
picture is the valuable and rare specimen; the ordinary one
was just picked up to match.

73. Left-handed Whelk (*Busycon contrarium Conrad*) and, right, the
almost impossible-to-find right-handed specimen to match.

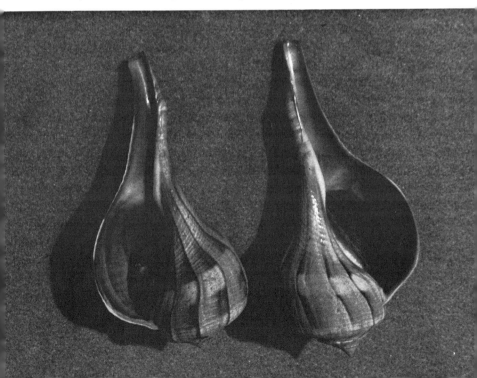

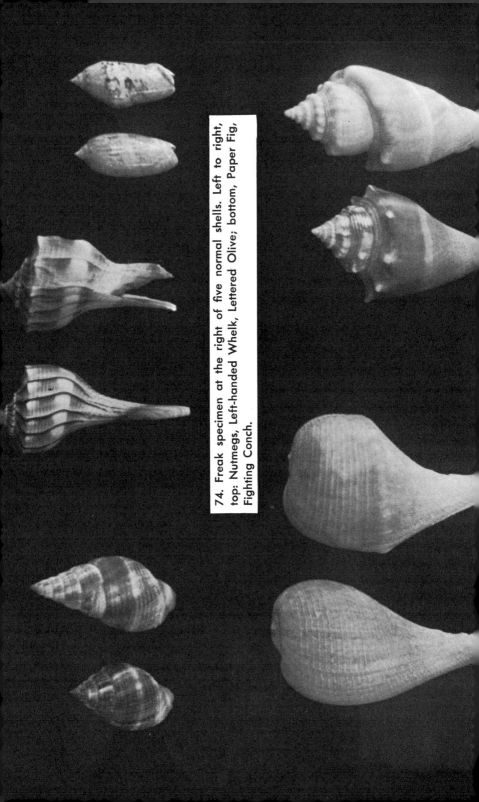

74. Freak specimen at the right of five normal shells. Left to right, top: Nutmegs, Left-handed Whelk, Lettered Olive; bottom, Paper Fig, Fighting Conch.

You will find many, many other freak specimens, some of which are illustrated on page 192. Note the Left-handed Whelk with two tails—two siphonal canals—for instance. The monetary worth of such a find probably is not great; still, some collectors value these specimens highly and might be willing to pay a lot to own one which particularly appealed.

In the illustration the freak shell is on the right. At the left, top row, is a Nutmeg (*Cancellaria reticulata Linné*) which somehow lost its spire. At the top of the body whorl you can see a light area with a crack around it. This is what's left of the original spire. In building a new one the mollusk got carried away with its work and built it much higher than the original had been.

Next is the Left-handed Whelk; a repair was needed and the animal evidently figured that such an area should join a siphonal canal. So it made a new one on the repair and ended up with two.

The Lettered Oliva (*Oliva sayana Ravenal*) somehow got off on the wrong mantle and gave itself a ridge. On the lower line, left, the Paper Fig (*Ficus communis Röding*) got itself a ridge and a twisted lower half. And the Fighting Conch (*Strombus alatus Gmelin*), the most interesting of all these, also lost its spire. Then, faced either with a repair job of magnitude or death, the animal inside put on a new spire after a fashion. But obviously he didn't know how to build just a spire. This is the first thing built by a univalve and is of course actually drawn out in a spiral rather than built in the ordinary sense. So he did all he knew to do; he built a new small shell to plug the gap. As you can see, it perches up there, a perfect shell on top of a big shell. It gets the job done. In the case of a Fighting Conch, as with some other mollusks, the young shell is a slightly different shape from the one which the full-grown shell assumes. In fixing the damage, this Fighting Conch reverted to early life and built a young-conch-shaped shell to fill the gap in the old-conch-shaped shell in which he was living.

The most common type of freak shell comes from damage

75. This Fighting Conch patched a large hole right in the middle of his shell.

76. A mended Banded Tulip shell

77. A Fighting Conc mended three times

to the mollusk inside and its attempt to repair that damage. These tiny creatures can do incredible repair work with their calcium-forming mantle. Several examples are shown above. You can see where the Fighting Conch on the left had lost more than two square inches of its shell and somehow repaired the damage. The line of demarcation between the new and the old is very plain. He didn't bother much with the outside appearance; the mend isn't even the same color as the original shell. But the inside, where the body would feel it, is smooth and perfect.

The Banded Tulip (*Fasciolaria hunteria Perry*) shows a less discernible line of mend. But you can plainly tell where it is because the cross bands on the new don't meet or match the old. And the other Fighting Conch on the right has mended his shell not once but three times. I found the shell dead; if it had still been alive I would never have had the heart to take it after it had apparently fought so hard for its life.

One of the puzzling aspects of this matter concerns how the damage in these cases was inflicted. If a huge fish had crushed the shell, it would have consumed the animal inside. It is hard to conceive a blow heavy enough to break the shell; a Fighting Conch has a strong, heavy shell, and water slows up and tends to smother any sort of blow. About the only thing left would be some sort of falling object, and it would have had to be very, very heavy to have inflicted the damage. Perhaps a shrimper's net could have been responsible.

We have two shelled mollusks whose habits and abilities are so outstanding that they should be mentioned in this chapter. One is a camouflage expert and one is a marine architect.

The camouflage expert is the Carrier Shell (*Xenophora*), which we have already mentioned in passing. This animal collects old pieces of shell, even whole shells, and maneuvers them up onto its own shell and cements (or calciums) them in place there. It doesn't do this job all at once; it is a lifetime proposition. It adds a shell each time it draws out its own shell lip. Thus the top-shaped shell itself is never in view, only the pile of old debris.

The chances are it takes whatever is handy at the time, but this is not certain because our own American species, the Atlantic Carrier Shell (*Xenophora conchyliophora Born*), uses mostly single valves of bivalves. It may be just that bivalves are handy or it could be that when one is needed the animal searches out an appropriate-sized valve that's just right for the purpose. Mr. DeMarco in his Florida Marine Museum at Fort Myers has a Carrier Shell in which bivalves and univalves were alternated by the tiny camouflage expert. Perhaps the original owner had an orderly, systematic complex as part of his character. The specimen we have photographed seems only to have been working for that good safe pile-of-old-shells look.

The marine architect is the Purple Snail Shell, known by the Latin name of *Janthina*. There are several species, but

78. Predator-killed shells. In each case you can see how the attacker bored through the shell to get at its victim.

79. Carrier Shell (*Xenophora*). Note the way the mollusk cements pieces of shell onto his shell for camouflage.

the most common on both coasts of the United States is the Common Purple Janthina (*Janthina janthina Linné*).

This is a shell shaped a lot like the Cat's Eye and the Tiger's Eye. It is about an inch in length, rounded, light bluish-purple on top and a deep purple-lilac toward the bottom.

This creature spends its entire lifetime floating around in warm water on the surface. It builds for this purpose a very efficient raft that looks like a glob of cellophane which you've taken off a candy box and wadded up for the waste basket.

It manufactures this raft by encasing tiny bubbles of air in a mucus-type material which hardens in air and sea water. The bubbles are stuck together, and the whole raft is fastened to the foot of the Janthina.

The animal doesn't sit on its raft; it hangs from the underside of it where it functions as a weighted keel. When the time comes to lay eggs the Janthina lays them against the underside of the raft, and they are thus protected from the sun and weather.

This mollusk enjoys warm water, but goes wherever winds and currents take it. The Gulf Stream sometimes carries it so far north that it is washed up with dozens of its fellows on the beaches of Massachusetts and Connecticut. Mostly, though, storms drive it ashore if at all on the beaches of our southermost states.

In addition to the mucus for building its raft the Janthina secretes a purple dye which it sometimes exudes when it is washed up on shore. If thousands of these shells are washed up, often the sands are dyed purplish. It will stain your fingers when you pick one of the animals up.

So here we have a seagoing marine mollusk that designs and builds a fine raft, just what it needs for roaming the vast areas of the ocean, sometimes never seeing land in its lifetime.

All these together are the valuable shells, the freak shells, the unusual animals. They only add to the interest in the vast world of mollusks.

15

Miniatures, Albinos, Fossils

SHELL collectors start off with only big shells. Then gradually discrimination comes to them in what they pick up and keep.

There is one further step; when the collector has become very sophisticated indeed, has begun to turn the nose up slightly at beach-collected specimens, and when he converses about shells primarily in Latin, then comes the miniature collection.

The rank amateur can be forgiven if he thinks, the first time he is shown a collection of miniatures, that probably all room in the collector's house for any more of the larger shells is gone and therefore he has *had* to turn to the tiny specimens. Perhaps there is even a germ of truth in that idea.

Mainly, though, people turn to miniatures because in them it is possible to make the greatest showing in the smallest space. And because it presents a further challenge when the collector has gone about as far as he can go in improving his collection of regular-sized shells. Obviously if you try to collect a miniature of every shell you have in your regular collection, at least as much work will have to be expended to be successful as was expended in the first place, and probably a whole lot more.

Again from the amateur's point of view, one of the most interesting things about the collecting of miniatures is the posture of anyone on the beach collecting them.

You have to get your face down as low as your knees in order to see the little things. The older you are, the truer this is. You do this by spreading the legs slightly and bending forward from the waist, the rear elevated sharply. Some of the larger, more rotund of the miniature collectors, headed north, present a rather striking picture to anyone south of them. A beach full of miniature gatherers is an interesting sight and looks a little like a group of ostriches trying in time-honored fashion to hide their heads in the sand.

This is an entirely different type of shell collecting. You handle the shells mostly with tweezers, and use a magnifying glass to examine what you are working on. Some collectors have a glass set in an adjustable metal stand so that they can have both hands free to work on and clean a given shell, and at the same time see it under magnification.

You beach-collect miniatures bent over, as I've said. When you find a patch that seems productive, you can sit or lie down and look everything over carefully. Usually in the sun's bright light you don't need a glass to show you what's there. But you'll need it later in the house.

With only a few exceptions (the main one of which is the shape-changing cowries), you can find tiny specimens of most shells. I have seen cones and pectens so small I could hardly pick them out. Yet when I examined them under magnification they were perfect.

Once in looking over a lot of tiny shells at the inside edge of the swash channel at minus tide, my wife and I found two tiny perfect Lady's Ears. They were about an eighth of an inch in diameter and we bought a domed magnifying holder to display them. This suddenly struck me as absurd; to strive to get such a tiny specimen and then buy a magnifying dome to make it large enough to be seen, a size you might have been able to find more easily in the first place. Still I did just that.

There is, of course, no limit to what you can do with miniatures. There is always a chance, even after your collection is fairly complete, of finding an even smaller specimen of a miniature you already have and substituting it.

As I say, the majority of miniatures are collected on the beach by people bending, sitting, or lying there with their faces close to the shells they are examining. But there is another way to get them. That is by buying mud in bags or baskets brought in from deep water, and then going over it literally with a comb.

Such mud, because of collecting and transporting costs, is very expensive. It costs somewhere around $5 a bushel. But if you are just interested in miniatures you can buy mud cheaper from which all the larger shells have been screened with a quarter-inch mesh screen. The saving is considerable, and what is left after the screening is strictly for the miniature collection.

There are wonderful finds reported. A next-door neighbor of mine used to pore over bushels of this mud evening after evening at a table on his porch. I saw a number of Lemon Pectens he had found that were less than an eighth of an inch, and still were perfect both in color and shape.

Interested collectors sometimes carry the mud north from southern beaches when they go, and in the remaining winter evenings invite shell-gathering friends in for "mud parties" at which they have a delightfully messy time going over the stuff.

One miniature collection which I saw in a glassed coffee table had a tremendous number of perfect little shells, many that I had never seen before in miniature. And the owner had a reading glass fastened to the edge of the table with a small detachable chain so that you could examine what you were seeing.

In the same category with miniatures are the albinos. This presents a different and even rougher challenge. These are freaks or sports which are exactly like the regular shell but are pure white. They make a very impressive showing displayed against a black background, all without a spot of color.

The amateur, again, is impressed no end the first time he sees such a collection. But in the back of his mind there is a question; has he been overlooking hundreds of these on a beach covered primarily with white shells, through ignorance of their value, or are they as hard to find as everyone seems to think?

Actually, many of those white shells that cover the beach are not all white. And others are always white (like some arks) and are very plentiful to boot. Colored shells fade in the sun after a long, long time and look almost white. But to find an albino Banded Tulip or a Chinese Alphabet Cone in pure white might mean the search of a lifetime.

You should make your albino collection (and your miniature collection, for that matter) concurrent with your regular collection. It is less frustrating that way. Always be on the lookout for the lovely albino, and when on rare occasions you do find one, keep it in a special place. When you have enough to make a showing, you can work on them. You can catalog from the notes you have stuffed into the aperture, and display them handsomely.

The trick to it comes in always having albinos in the back of your mind so that when you come upon a lovely pure white cockle on a beach full of white shells, your eye won't pass over it just because it is the cockle shape and because cockles are everywhere. Or when you see a pure white Fighting Conch on a white beach it will register in your mind even though you have more Fighting Conchs than you know what to do with.

The third form of special collection is the fossil collection. And this is completely different from the other two. The possibilities are limitless, but it will mean work and travel and luck to put together an interesting fossil collection.

Some of these fossilized shells are many thousands of years old. Specimens fifteen feet long whose animals are now extinct have been dug up. There are thousands of species which today exist only in fossil form. And there are variations of

80. Fossil specimens from a digging near Tice, Florida

shells we know today which no one has ever seen except in fossil form.

It means work to collect these, because digging must be done by someone, somewhere. If it isn't done by you, it will have to be done by someone for you, or you will have to take advantage of digging which someone is doing for some other purpose. It will mean travel because the places where it is possible to dig successfully for fossil shells are seldom in your neighborhood. And the luck comes in finding helpful excavating going on.

Indian mounds can contain, but don't necessarily have to contain, fossil shells. Archeological expeditions turn them up, or find them in tombs. I know of a man who found fossil shells in the excavated material from an office-building cellar in New York City.

Seashore road building or canal building is very productive. This is especially true in Florida where the entire state is so very close to sea level and was inundated for centuries. Wonderful finds have been made when power shovels have been excavating, especially in the Lake Okeechobee area.

Between Tice and Alva, Florida, several years ago, excavating was being done and we heard that fine fossil specimens were being uncovered with each shovelful. Mrs. Hoyt went with a carload of Sanibel shell collectors, and the digging lived up to advance rumor completely.

They scraped in the dirt already loosened or removed, or sometimes it was possible to reach up and remove fossil shells which had been partly uncovered in the sheer walls of the excavation. The shelling party had a fabulous time, and came home with so many fossil shells that the springs of the car sagged.

I have said that Junonias are extremely hard to find. It must have been different millions of years ago, because in that small excavation my wife alone found fourteen fossil Junonias. Fossil shells have for the most part a chalky appearance (though this does not always hold; the party was astonished to find that the olives retained much of their sheen). The color was gone. There was no mistaking the Junonia shape. And on several specimens we thought we could detect the spots. Some of these fossils are shown on page 202.

There are, then, challenging fringe areas in the collecting of shells. Two of these—miniatures and albinos—can and should be carried on at the same time you are building your regular collection. But the third, fossil collecting, is a completely different type of endeavor and must be carried on in a competely different way.

16

Processing Shells

AFTER you have collected your shells, especially your live specimens, you have to take care of them. Some people look upon this part of the hobby as drudgery; others find it fascinating. It depends on whether or not you enjoy working with your hands and whether or not you have a painstaking nature.

Fortunately a lot of shell collectors, over the years, have experimented and by trial and error have evolved a set of rules which you can follow.

First off you must remove the animal from the shell you have collected. If you don't, after a short time either the shell or you will have to leave the house.

Furthermore you should remove it at once because if you don't the animal may die and harden inside to the point where nothing can remove him. This you can get around by keeping the shell in water, but here again a note of caution; if the shell is allowed to stand in water without the water being changed quite often, the acids given off by the dead animal may spoil the luster of the shell. Your laboriously collected, bright specimen will look more drab even than a not-too-good beach-collected specimen.

The most common method for killing the animal and removing the body is to boil the specimen for about five minutes. You'll need to boil very large univalves much longer than that, of course. A very large one might require boiling for half an hour.

If your specimen is a bivalve, you have little problem. When the animal is killed by the boiling water, the adductor muscle relaxes, and the hinge automatically opens the two valves of the shell and leaves them agape. You simply scrape out the body of the animal, using care not to harm the inside of the shell itself.

With a univalve you have a different proposition. The animal's body is wrapped around the columella and no amount of boiling is going to unwrap it and bring it out. Furthermore it is imperative to perform the operation before the body cools from the boiling or it will "set." As soon as you can comfortably handle the shell is the time.

The tool you use for the removal can be anything: a long piece of stiff wire with a hook on the end, an ice pick, an appropriate dental tool, a crochet hook. Anything your ingenuity dreams up will be fine.

Usually you can insert this tool past the operculum after boiling the animal. But sometimes it is too tightly in place to do so without damaging either it or the shell. In that case you should insert a thin-blade knife and gradually cut the muscle and raise the operculum until it can be removed. I have found that a curve-bladed grapefruit knife, doctored with a pair of pliers to bend the end even more, is very efficient.

You drive the removal instrument from the siphonal canal side as far into the flesh of the animal as you can, and twist a little to set it if it has a hook on the end. Then you hold the instrument in one hand and the shell in the other and "unscrew" the animal from inside.

I realize that this sounds absurd, but that is exactly the motion you use. After all, you're unwinding the body from around the columella. And you must operate gently, not using undue force if it sticks. Because once you break off an end by forcing, you have no further contact with that end and it will cause you a whole lot more work before you can get it out. It is better, when it won't come easily, to put it back in the pot and boil it a little more than to try to cope with the horror of that remaining decomposing end.

On page 156 we show a picture of a large Left-handed Whelk from which the body, shown beside it, was removed intact. You will see the huge operculum still attached to the foot and the coils of the body.

Boiling may damage high-sheen shells like cowries and olives, even crack them. To guard against this, always start your shells in lukewarm water and bring the water very slowly to a boil. Then allow it slowly to cool until it is lukewarm again.

Even with this treatment and meticulous care, you sometimes harm these highly polished shells. And so some shellers with shiny shells (and some with all their shells) use the water method. In this you leave the shells in water, changing the water two or three times a day. And each time, you try to flush out as much of the body as possible under the tap before you return the shell to the container. As the flesh softens and gradually deteriorates, the flushing will remove more and more of it until the shell is finally clean. This is a long, messy and stomach-turning process, and only the most painstaking want to be bothered with it.

There are other methods, used mostly with small shells. One is to soak the animal in alcohol for a few days. This gets rid of the odor but not the animal. You could afford to trust only a very small univalve to remain odorless. Another drawback to this method is that the alcohol makes the body contract violently in some cases, and this pulls the operculum clear in out of sight. If this should happen you have lost the shell completely. If the animal is dead or almost dead before the soaking starts, this will probably not be a problem.

For small shells, a much simpler method is to leave the shells lying out on the ground, preferably near an anthill.

Ants and blowflies will take care of the situation for you. But it is well to have an understanding wife, family, and set of neighbors if you live on a narrow lot. This method is also the best way to rid yourself of that broken-off end which I mentioned above.

If it is too earthy for you, though, the alcohol soaking method is probably your answer. Some collectors use formaldehyde to embalm the remainder. But if very much is left up in there, success is "iffy." And believe me you have no idea what iffy success in such an endeavor can mean until you try to drive north in cold weather with the car windows closed and one of these partial failures in the back seat with you. If you ever see a large whelk beside the road in Maryland where no whelk ought to be, it may be my monument to such an experience at the point where I gave up. Boiling, then, is simplest; ants are best for the small shells or remainders. Formaldehyde should be used in about a four-percent solution instead of the usual forty-percent.

There is one pitfall. Sometime during your first efforts along these lines you are going to boil and remove the animals from a fairly large batch of shells and you are going to realize when the whole process is over that you have no faintest idea which operculum goes with which shell. This usually happens to you when you are boiling up shells that are all approximately the same size, but it can happen with any set of shells because some opercula don't fit their openings very well.

All I can do is warn you that this will happen and suggest a couple of ways of avoiding it. Immediately upon removal of the animal's body and the cutting of the operculum from the foot, label it and its shell with duplicate-numbered bits of adhesive tape. Then there will be no problem. If you are leaving the shell out for the ants, the operculum will have been cut off first; thus it is especially important to design some system for linking it with the correct shell.

Once you have the shell completely clean on the inside,

you have to decide what you want to do with the outside crustings, barnacles, dirt, periostracum and other things which are on it.

If you are an ordinary collector you will want to remove all this and bring out the lovely coloring or sheen or both of the shell itself. But if you are a scientist you may be one of those who feels a shell is not a shell without the periostracum intact. Perhaps if you have several specimens your best course is to leave one in its natural state with periostracum and clean all the others.

Cleaning methods are about as many as there are shell enthusiasts. Some people use Clorox, some use muriatic acid and some scrape. To my mind, scraping is easiest and the least dangerous. Lots of times barnacles will snap away easily when a knife blade is used. Dirt will give up to soap and water and a brush; everybody has an old toothbrush hanging around that can be pressed into service.

If after scraping and cleaning there is still film, soak the shell in a Clorox solution. Very often this will dissolve whatever is on it and bring out the true colors of the shell. Some shellers swear by a twenty-percent solution of bleach, some want more, and there are a few who use it full strength. If you use it too strong and leave it too long, you probably won't hurt the shell itself, but you may very well impair its bright coloring. The answer in my case is to use the stuff full strength and then watch the shell carefully and take it out and wash it as soon as the film is gone. In this way, if you have to keep it in there a long time and you harm the coloring, you have the consolation of knowing that it wouldn't have been much good to you in its un-Cloroxed state anyway. You have to take a chance on stubborn stains.

If the specimen is not terribly valuable or important to you, it can be left in a weaker solution overnight. Some kinds of shells stand soaking better than others; the worst one of all is the Carrier Shell, which is likely to lose, if you soak it, the pile-of-old-shells look which makes it valuable. The calcium which tacks the old pieces of shell in place can be dissolved along with calcium deposits you *are* trying to get rid of, and the results are disasterous.

The muriatic-acid bit is dangerous both for you and the shell, though it is used all the time. The very existence of the tables with their places for acid bottles outside the houses on shell beaches bears silent witness to this fact.

About all I can say is that in most cases it isn't needed and you would be better off without it. Don't be swayed by all the wise talk about using acid unless you are sure of the knowledge and ability of the person doing the talking.

If you can't remove stains any other way, though, then paint a little on the stubborn place and wash off under running water instantly. If the results are good, try another larger spot that needs it. If the results are not good you haven't ruined your whole shell; the place you experimented on is probably no worse than it was to start with.

Remember, acid will burn. You should use chemists' tongs or the equivalent, and never pick up the shell being treated or hold it in your fingers. Have a strong baking-soda solution ready in case you want instantly to neutralize the acid with a base on yourself or the shell. Mostly running water will take the acid off, but a base is faster. And if it gets on you, speed is vital. Don't leave the bottle anywhere where young children can get at it even by climbing. You could ruin a child's whole life by not taking care in this area. If at all possible, work with an expert the first time you use acid.

You will probably hear about dipping your shell in straight or half-strength muriatic acid. I can conceive of shells in such an extreme condition that this would be necessary once or twice in a lifetime. If you have such a case, dip the shell and remove it instantly, upright to keep the acid from being held inside the apex where it might eat through before water or soda could reach it. Remember, muriatic eats the calcium which the shell is made of along with the excrescences you are trying to remove.

A very weak solution will sometimes brighten the colors

of an old beach-worn specimen by removing the deteriorated layer of calcium on the outside. Masons get the same effect by washing a stone chimney they have just finished with a muriatic-acid solution to bring out the colors of the stones. Again, the word which can't be repeated too often is "care." Use care in every contact with acid.

All experts I've talked with agree that you should never use lacquer or varnish or any such material on shells. It brightens the shell, but artificially, and spoils it as a scientific specimen if you or anyone you turn the collection over to should want to use it for study.

Opinion isn't anywhere near so unanimous in regard to baby oil or a high-grade machine oil. A lot of collectors will have nothing to do with it, but an equal number rub their specimens with an oily rag, inside and out. These people have a very persuasive argument. First off the oil makes the shell look brighter; a wet shell will always look brighter than a dry one and an oiled shell will hold that same look indefinitely. But in addition, these scientists claim that sunlight and Clorox and washing dry out the thousands of minute pigment-oil particles in the calcium which gave the shell its color. If you keep oil on the shell it not only protects against further deterioration, but actually penetrates and replaces the dried-up oil and thus brings the colors to life again.

Certainly it sounds reasonable, and certainly shells do look better oiled, but there is one major drawback. You have to have shells covered somehow from the dust if you adopt this custom. A dry shell is easy to dust. An oiled shell just adds the dust to the coating of oil and pretty soon you have a double-dyed mess. But shells in glass cases or under plastic present no problem and remain bright.

There are all sorts of tools suggested by various people for this work. One man advocates one of those outfits that have attachments for buffing and for grinding. This is a machine age and such an outfit may be fine in the hands of someone who knows exactly how to use it. I can believe, though, that sometimes in grinding off bits of unwanted material you might hold the whirling grinder or burr against the spot too long and come up with a hole in the shell. But there is no denying that use of such a machine would be easier than the old hand-scraping.

Still, that has worked fairly well for centuries. You can use a kitchen knife or any tool in a hardware store that appeals to you as something you need to solve a particular problem in your cleaning. But the very best instruments in my opinion are an old set of discarded dental tools.

A next-door neighbor of mine had such a set of tools. They have shapes that allow you to do almost anything and get into almost any crevice. If you are lucky enough to find such a set at a reasonable figure, you will clean shells expertly, quickly and well. A not-too-pleasant job will be made much more pleasant.

When the cleaning is finished and the shell is ready, stuff the opening with cotton. And you can either glue the operculum to the cotton, leaving it in its proper place in the opening, or you can wrap it in tissue paper or Kleenex and insert that, too, in the opening with the cotton. The shell now is ready for cataloging and housing.

We find, then, that preparing the shells for their place in polite society after you have collected them often takes as much work as, or more work than, the original collecting. The right tools and materials help in this work. And knowing the pitfalls helps, too.

17

Cataloging and Housing Shells

ONE important thing is to make sure you catalog and house your shells according to some pre-thought-out system that appeals to *you*. Actually it doesn't matter much what direction the system takes as long as it is a fairly complete system, aims in the direction you as a collector want to go, and as long as it has complete records. You'll just have to take my word for the importance of records until you can stay with the hobby long enough to discover for yourself their need, their ease, and their importance in your own case.

If you think about it a little, the absurdity is apparent in going to the trouble of collecting a lot of interesting, even valuable shells, and then haphazardly filling old cartons with them and relegating the cartons to the cellar or the attic. Even if you do get the cartons out sometime, you're going to forget where you got the shells, possibly even their identity if you ever knew it. And someday your heirs, swearing mightily, are going to carry the cartons to the dump.

I can't advise too strongly that you get a notebook (preferably loose-leaf so you can type the entries) and make a catalog. All you have to do is number each shell you collect. Then you attach a tiny bit of adhesive tape (or anything else you find better) to the shell with the number on it. Then you write the number into the notebook-catalog together with what information you have on the identity of the shell, the circumstances of its collection, and the spot in the collection where you have housed it.

From this crude start you can refine your system in any direction you want to go. If you are going to be a very serious, scientific collector with an ambition to make your collection of as much value to the world of learning as possible, the more information and detail you can furnish, the better. You would want to prepare the collection in such a way that it could be left to a museum or library and the person receiving it would know almost as much about each of your shells as you yourself knew at the time you collected them.

If, on the other hand, you had no such ambitions, the minimum information I have suggested above might be sufficient for you. However, often in the past lukewarm collectors have changed to red-hot collectors as they got further and further into it. And if such were the case with you, you might then be embarrassed at the scarcity of detail in your early gatherings.

I would therefore recommend a lot more than the minimum no matter what your present intentions are. You could, with very little trouble, add information about whether the specimen was beach collected, shallow- or deep-water collected, whether it was alive, just dead, or dead with no animal inside. If it was alive you could well add information on what it was doing at the time you found it. Was it eating, hiding, boring into another mollusk's shell? What was the time of day or night? What was the day of the month and the year? What was the weather like? What was the tide?

This information and more like it you could put either in the catalog or on the card that you keep with the shell. Personally I lean toward the catalog. Cards can get lost but a catalog has everything in one place. And the number attached to the shell probably won't get lost.

If there should be any habit or characteristic which you discovered when you found the shell, something you had not known about before, by all means this should be added. In the matter of place of collection, you should pinpoint the place exactly. It should not be simply "Florida," nor even "Sanibel Island, Florida." It should be "One quarter mile east of Woodring Point, Bay side of Sanibel Island, Florida, February 16, 1966, 4:30 P.M. in two feet of water at mean tide, eating a clam." You can use even more information than that if it is pertinent. But that gives you an idea. It doesn't take long to type two or three extra lines in the catalog and it makes all the difference. If yours is a really scientific effort use India ink instead of typing and special paper guaranteed to last for centuries.

You should add identity of the shell, or leave space for it if you don't know it. If you know only the common name, fine; use that. But as soon as possible add the Latin name so that you will have both.

To identify shells that are strange to you, you must work with published shell catalogs and illustrated guides to shells. In my opinion the standard guide to the shells of North and Central America and the Caribbean area is *American Seashells* by R. Tucker Abbot. Dr. Abbot occupies the Pilsbry Chair of Malacology, Academy of Natural Sciences in Philadelphia, Pennsylvania. His is a big, complete book. Most shell collectors own their own copies.

There are so many different shells that admittedly the job is sometimes tough. This is especially true among the bivalves where the only distinction between kinds is sometimes the hinges and their hinge teeth. But it is nowhere near as hard as it would be if you couldn't eliminate so many kinds right at the start. If the shell is a bivalve, you have immediately eliminated all univalves from consideration and that is more than half the battle right there. Then if you decide it has the scallop shape you are bringing the problem down into a manageable area.

Next, if it has one valve flat and the other rounded, you have eliminated all but the fans. You found the shell on a Georgia beach, and so you eliminate all fans from the Pacific and of course the lovely, huge fans from Japan.

You examine the descriptions of the ones that could have

come from Georgia. You hope it might be Ravenel's Scallop because that is a rare one, but you read that that one has about 25 ribs where your shell has only 19. You find that the more common Zigzag Scallop is listed as having between 18 and 20 ribs, and you have hit that right on the nose with your specimen. So you come to the conclusion you have a Zigzag Scallop (*Pecten ziczac Linné*) and so name it. Eliminating got you to your final conclusion fairly quickly. The Venus clams, the tellens, the arks are more difficult perhaps, but the same rules apply. If everything else fails you, turn the bivalve so that you are looking down at the hinge area, and almost without exception you will see the difference even in shells that appear identical in other ways.

Univalves are, in my opinion, much easier to identify than bivalves. The various species differ radically enough in most cases so that the differences are obvious even to the layman. So, identity is an interesting game even when it is difficult, as it often is. You get a great deal of satisfaction out of your successes. Other shell collectors like to play the game, too, and they will give you help in stubborn cases. Even some museum curators love their work and all shells in general, and are so interested in both and are so nice that they will help when all other sources fail you. But there are differences among curators just as there are among all other people, and you may strike one who has been imposed upon or is especially busy at that time. In any event, you should bend over backward never to ask help from such professionals except as a last resort, and never to impose by running to them often.

Housing comes next. And here again many factors enter in. First is the amount of space available.

It is a pretty good rule of thumb that whatever space you have will be multiplied many times if you use drawers of some sort and somehow in this way manage to stack containers of shells one above the other.

The ideal is a custom-made chest with different-height drawer trays. It is possible to have this extend up to eye level, and this allows you to house a great many shells. The purpose of having the drawers of different heights is, of course, because some shells are big and some small. Some drawers must house a Triton's Conch or a huge Left-handed Whelk while others need be no more than half an inch high to house tiny univalves or the flat valves of bivalves displayed butterfly-wise. Those who want to be completely meticulous use plastic or glass vials for their smallest shells and place a few vials in each drawer.

Or you can have your shell chest made waist-high, the top made of glass so that always the top tray will be on display under glass. A waist-high shell chest also allows you to place upon it one of the lower trays which you have pulled out to examine or show.

A battery of such chests in a room recess or along one full side of a room, with bright (possibly florescent) light above it, is extremely effective. The front of each drawer should have some easy-identification tag in a little holder so that by looking at the catalog and then at the tag you can lay your hands instantly on any shell you own. While you are building such chests, it costs very little to add some method of locking them.

If you are middle-aged or better, your basement may be your answer to the area you use. The area that was once a rumpus room when the kids were home lends itself to re-doing as a shell room once their ping-pong table and other equipment is put away. If you are younger and have a den, possibly one wall of the den is your answer. Some attics lend themselves to refinishing as a shell room. If you are in your teens, one wall of your own room is a possibility.

If you have no money for a custom-made chest system, your answer may be a series of second-hand chests from the discards of relatives, thread cases which a department store may give away, or shipping cases or cartons which you can fit out with cut cardboard dividers. Ingenuity and improvisation will many times take the place of money and give you storage space which even the opulent collectors may envy.

If you have a small collection or plenty of room or both, clothing stores will sometimes save for you and give you sweater boxes which have a transparent plastic cover. These are ideal for your purpose and will display a considerable number of shells depending on size, especially if fitted with cardboard dividers. These boxes can then be displayed on that no-longer-used ping-pong table that was once the kids'. The shells are all viewable and yet are protected from dust. If you are handy with tools, at a very small cost you can make a frame for such boxes and slide them into it like drawers, to cut down the space your shells are taking up.

White cotton batting makes a nice lining for drawers or boxes, but should be covered with a sheet of waxed paper or plastic because otherwise the cotton fibers may stick to the shells. A plain black cloth is another fine background, especially for white shells or albinos.

Each shell should have its name on a card or label Scotch-taped to the background under it. Personally I think it should have both the common and Latin names, but purists are horrified by any use of the common name. To me it is an imposition on non-shell-collecting friends, who may want to look at your collection, to leave these people completely in the dark about the shells. And let's face it, that's what you do if you use only Latin titles.

In my opinion you should, too, increase the impact of your collection for those who see it by adding to the cards unusual information which the layman would consider interesting. An explanation of the Carrier Shell, for instance, would interest any viewer. Or a note like this would score: "Textile Cone (*Conus textile Linné*). This cone is often mistaken for the fabulously valuable Glory-of-the-Seas Cone. Its mollusk is venomous; it has a poison barb with which it can pump potent poison into a victim. Textile Cones have been known to kill people." Even the very blasé would be interested in such a notation.

You may choose to house and display your shells by families, by size, by countries, by regions, by areas you have shelled, or in any other way convenient for you. If you are specializing in one type of shell—volutes, pectens, cones or any other—you would probably find that displaying your shells by species would suit your purposes best. Many times collectors find some special shell type that interests them and choose to try to get all the shells of that shell type rather than to get representatives of all types from all over the world.

Some books suggest mounting shells on cardboard with a drop of glue. Again, personally I think this is a great mistake. If you do this you never do see the back of your shell again, and getting the hardened glue off is next to impossible if you want to move the shell or upgrade your collection with a better specimen and trade the old one. It is fine to mount duplicates in this way to hang as wall ornaments; they are most decorative. But you won't be able to protect them from dust unless you lay them flat, and if you lay them flat they might as well not be glued. Shell novelty places often offer frames and the round magnifying dome holders, any of which are fine for a limited number of duplicates.

In the same way the glass-topped coffee table and the shelved room dividers which you see so often in shell beach cottages and in the homes of shell collectors are fine display cases for special shells under glass. Or they are ideal for displaying a whole shell family for a while, then changing to another family when your friends have all got a bit sick of seeing that first one. They are, in other words, fine for the display of part of a collection, but not a good place to keep all your shells. Even if your collection is very small, it will look crowded in even the biggest coffee table. Keep your shells in a chest, cataloged, and display certain shells from it in your coffee table or display case. A selection of albinos, next month miniatures, then Florida shells, next California shells, next foreign shells, will keep these display areas interesting both to you and your family, and to your guests.

We find, then, that cataloging is not much work, and pays

fabulous dividends in time saved and confusion overcome. And that the catalog should refer you to drawers in some sort of chest or case where your shells can lie safe, away from dust and sunshine, yet at your immediate call.

18

Mollusks with an Impact
on the Economy

I DISCUSSED the tremendous impact which mollusks had
in the past on the course of world events. This impact was
not confined to past centuries; it is with us today. Historians
in ages to come will have to evaluate it fully, which is of
necessity impossible for us to do now.

Still, areas of that impact are clear even today. There are
many businesses, whole towns and whole areas that base
their economic well-being on mollusks. Many skilled persons spend their productive lives dealing with mollusks and
with molluscan enemies, with the preparation of mollusks
for the table, with the preparation of their shells or their
pearls for ornamentation. Scientists study them, their needs,
their life patterns, how to protect them, their remaining
skeletons. Governments make laws regarding their sale and
consumption, set up agencies to enforce these laws, and in
addition set up and assign ocean areas to operators to "farm"
certain mollusks. Law-enforcement agents afloat and ashore
deal with poachers on these assigned areas.

And lastly, those who consume mollusks as food have
their diet and life habits influenced, even if only mildly, by
this consumption.

As far as we can know today, the oyster holds the greatest
role of all the mollusks upon our economic stage. The Long
Island Sound oyster industry alone, before it was hit by a

starfish invasion in 1957, produced oysters worth $7,000,000 dockside each year. And the Long Island industry is only one segment of the oyster industry of the United States. Chesapeake Bay produces more oysters than Long Island Sound. Pacific Coast oystering areas produce fabulous takes of oysters.

Any business involving mollusks and millions of dollars packs interest for shell collectors. The life cycle of an oyster is in itself interesting. And you must understand its life cycle before you can grasp completely the community impact we are speaking about. We'll examine it for Long Island Sound.

The oysters' spawning season there is governed by calendar and water temperature, and takes place about July 1. The eggs are discharged, fertilized, and larvae (called "spat") result. They are pelagic; they swim around and are carried by currents. Under the microscope you can see several waving feelers which they seem to use for swimming.

This pelagic state lasts about three weeks. Then the spat sink to the bottom and find something hard on which they can set up housekeeping for life. They prefer old oyster shells, but if they can't find any will accept something else. They attach themselves to one of these, grow, develop a shell of their own, and remain there always.

"Lots" in Long Island Sound are leased by the states of New York and Connecticut to oystermen. The Connecticut Shellfish Commission and the New York Conservation Department survey these lots and mark them with long cedar poles like telephone poles which are anchored at one end so that the other end sticks up out of water. These poles mark the corners of the lot the way a farmer marks the corners of his lot on land. These fields, though, are under water. To sail into such an area and see the poles sticking up on all sides is an experience. The oyster farmers, about July 1, spread thousands of bushels of old empty oyster shells over their lots to catch the spat when they are ready to attach. If eight or ten of the spat land on each shell, it is considered an ideal "set."

If starfish, drills, crabs, storms, silt or items of a like nature pass them by, the oysters grow large and eventually are harvested by the oystermen and end up on the half shell or in a stew.

Many things can happen to keep the eggs from fertilizing properly and the spat from setting if the eggs do hatch. Obviously many organisms feed on the spat. Lack of food, pollution, storms can be disastrous. There's nothing much you can do about a poor set except hope.

Starfish have been an oysterman's worst problem next to the poor set. This he could do something about. He used those mops we spoke about using to pick up mollusks in deep water. Only these were huge. These mops hang in a line on twenty-foot-long iron bars and are dragged, one on each side, by a mop boat.

The rope yarn entangles in the spines of the starfish. The whole thing is raised to the deck periodically and dunked into a long vat of boiling water, which kills the starfish. They become limp and drop off. One company, riding with the punch, has dried and silvered them for Christman-tree ornaments. Others have mixed them with seventy-five-percent trash fish and ground them up for chicken starter. They've even been used in fertilizer. And all the men who run the boats and make the mops and do all the other things, are having their lives influenced by a mollusk.

Starfish spawn about July 1, too. They, too, are pelagic for about the same length of time. Then they become starfish and start eating oysters. They do this by exerting the relentless pulling power that I described to you; then when they have opened the shell they eat the animal inside by extruding their own stomach inside the shell of the victim. They digest him right in his own home.

The Connecticut Shellfish Commission twice a year drags a small dredge bag along the bottom of Long Island Sound, always in the same areas, and by counting and tabulating the starfish caught, keeps track of how things are going.

In 1958 there was a prodigious oyster set. But in the fall previous, in 1957, when the starfish survey was taken, the Service found to their horror that the starfish, too, must have had a wonderful set. Because the very first bucket produced 1,439 starfish where seven had been taken six months earlier. Later results confirmed a thousand-percent increase overall in the starfish population just that summer.

Thus when the fine 1958 oyster set came along, that crawling army attacked gleefully and hungrily, and they didn't wait for the oysters to mature the way the oystermen had to, or for the month to have an R in it. Each starfish can consume several oysters a day, and one has, under ideal conditions, been known to eat six. You can imagine how long the set lasted with that going on.

The take from Long Island oystering dropped below $1,000,000. The U. S. Fish and Wildlife Service at Milford, Connecticut, under Dr. Victor L. Loosanoff, worked desperately to find a chemical which would kill starfish and not kill oysters or fish. He found that lime spread on the water and allowed to sink to the bottom made sores wherever it landed on a starfish, and later caused death. And he improved this finding later by impregnating sand with orthodichlorobenzene plus oil. This made worse sores if it touched a starfish, and could in addition to being spread be laid in a thick band around an area to keep starfish from coming back after the lot had once been treated. Starfish died if they tried to crawl across the barrier. This chemical and method have since been approved by the government.

But there has been no really good set of oysters since, and the companies are still hurting financially from the trouble starfish gave them in 1958. They can't afford to spend money to buy chemicals and treat ocean acreage when enough oysters haven't set to make it pay.

That's how matters stand now. In 1965 there was practically no set at all. If there should be a fine set now, the oystermen might be able to borrow money and protect this set with orthodichlorobenzene. As a by-product, the industry has always sold what oyster shells it produced. The principal uses for these (besides spreading to entice spat) have been in the feeding of calcium to chickens to make their eggshells hard. The oyster shells have also been used for road building.

Again, think of the number of people involved, the complexity and extent of the experiments, all revolving around a shelled mollusk. Then multiply that by all the oyster-producing areas in the world and you begin to get some idea of the vastness of the mollusk impact. Each area has its own problems that consist of set, enemies, and all the other things that can harrass. They aren't the same problems in each area, but they are just as real. In Chesapeake Bay, oyster pirates have operated over the beds at night for years and may still be operating. All these men and all this equipment and labor, even up to law-breaking, for just one mollusk.

Incidentally, if any reader has failed all his life to enjoy a first-class oyster stew he hasn't really lived. My advice is to search out a place that has a reputation for such a stew, or buy the oysters and search out a recipe or use the one at the end of this chapter. One such place that I personally can recommend unreservedly is the Oyster Bar downstairs below the waiting room in Grand Central Terminal in New York. The stew is produced by chefs while you sit at a counter and watch their every move. And it is completely delicious.

But eating oysters are not the only type that have their impact. Pearl oysters have produced pearls of magnificent luster, and natives have dived for them for centuries. Since their livelihood depends upon it, they think they have learned over these years how a pearl-harboring oyster may differ minutely in appearance from a nonpearl fellow.

Pearl oysters are, strictly speaking, not like oysters at all. They spend quite a bit of their lives mobile, and when they finally decide to come to rest permanently, they hitch themselves to the bottom not with calcium as do regular oysters but with a strong byssus. There are a number of different kinds of pearl oysters. It is said that a good "pearl man" can tell you just what part of the world any fine pearl came from. The type of mollusk, the salt and other content of the water, or the organisms on which the mollusk feeds, all have their influence on the pearl it produces.

Remember, the pearl is produced to cover up something which irritates the flesh of the animal inside the shell. It can be no more beautiful than the shell itself because the mollusk makes it with the same mantle and with the same material.

All mollusks can produce pearls to protect their flesh, but the golf-ball-size pearl of the Giant Clam looks chalky white like the inside of that huge creature's shell. The oysters we eat produce pearls and these are upon occasion found by diners. They look like the inside of an oyster shell and this isn't good from a financial point of view. And cooking spoils any value they might otherwise have had.

But there are valuable pearls produced by other mollusks. Abalones occasionally produce green or purple pearls which have considerable value. And the Queen Conch from the West Indies produces valuable pearls, too. But the shell from which you have the best chance of getting a valuable pearl in the United States is from the fresh-water clam. One such pearl was found many years ago in New Jersey. It was sold to a jeweler who shipped it abroad, where it became the property of Empress Eugénie. It was popularly known as the Queen Pearl and probably would be worth well over $25,000 today.

If the only return from the search for pearls were the pearl itself, the search wouldn't be in most cases financially feasible. But the pearl-bearing oyster shells (and even the fresh-water clam shells) that are thus gathered can be sold as mother-of-pearl for the making of buttons and ornaments.

The demand is prodigious. Thus there is an income constant, and any pearl that is found is a very welcome extra. Beds of fresh-water clams have been completely destroyed in areas of the Ohio River by this traffic.

Back in the old days, cameos were made from helmet shells or any shell with layers that were each of a different color or texture. The carving was done, and the rest of that layer removed so that the next layer became the background.

There are many areas of the world that produce pearl oysters from which, in turn, come lovely pearls. The Gulf of Persia and Ceylon are two of the most important. From this area the Hope Pearl, which weighed 1,800 pearl grains, is said to have come. Japan has many fine areas, as have China and the South Pacific islands. Pearls from the Bay of Panama are famous as is the mother-of-pearl industry there. Oriental pearls come from the Red Sea and seem to have a flamelike luster in the nacre. Because of this, that particular quality in a pearl is called its "orient."

One of the most famous sources of pearl oysters is the island of Margarita off the northern coast of Venezuela. The name means "pearl." Pearl Island. The very early Spaniards milked these island beds mercilessly and wastefully until they were depleted almost to the point of extinction. Those men made tremendous fortunes in doing so. The pearls in the Spanish royal crown came from these beds and the huge pearl in a Papal ring. Back in the early days when a dollar was worth many, many times what it is today, the yearly take from Margarita pearls was more than $6,000,000. Nowadays the pearl fisheries there have made an amazing comeback under the management of a company which has been given a lease to exploit these pearl fishing grounds. The company manages its take carefully and well, under approved conservation principles which will ensure the strength of the beds (and the income of the company) for the foreseeable future.

Pearl fishing, then, with its operations subsidized in many

cases by the more prosaic sale of mother-of-pearl, has been extremely lucrative and has given thousands upon thousands in many walks of life their livelihood.

However, it has been a most chancy undertaking. And man has never been one to leave matters to chance. The cultured-pearl industry grew from that fact. If oysters manufactured pearls around a bit of foreign matter that somehow got inside the shell, why not insert a foreign object and then put the oyster back in the water and let nature take its course?

The object which has proved best for insertion is a tiny bead cut from a fresh-water clam shell. These clams come from the United States and are found in the Mississippi River. Disease at one time attacked the beds of these clams and it was feared for a while that they might become extinct and the industry turn to different material. Tons ond tons of these clam shells have been shipped to Japan. There the Japanese cut the shells and thus make the tiny bead.

The bead, in turn, is inserted inside the folds of the mantle of a three-year-old Black-lipped Pearl Osyter (*Pinctada margaritifera Linné*) or a Japanese Pearl Oyster (*Pinctada mertensi Dunker*). And the oyster is returned to the water under controlled conditions.

Just exactly as he would if the irritation this provides came accidentally, the oyster covers the bead with layers of the same calcium carbonate that he used in making his shell. Since the pearl is in the mantle folds and nacre can be added on all sides, it is called a "free" pearl and is far more valuable than one produced, say, between the mantle and the shell itself. So "free" in this case certainly doesn't mean "for nothing."

When enough time has elapsed for the bivalve to complete the pearl, he is taken up again and opened. The resulting jewel is extracted. In some cases the pearl from that oyster is inserted in another for further development.

Let me stress, then, that cultured pearls are *not* artificial pearls. They are real pearls, formed by an oyster just like any other real pearl, but under controlled conditions with an artificial irritation stimulus and not in the wild state. They are just as beautiful, too, as wild-state pearls. But since the producer is not gambling the way a pearl diver gambles, and since the pearls are therefore cheaper to bring to market, easier to match perfectly, they are usually not as expensive as a wild-state pearl of the same size. A competent jeweler can tell with his instruments the difference in the core material. Artificial pearls, on the other hand, are man-made and are neither very valuable nor very beautiful.

Besides furnishing shells for artificial incentive to oysters to produce pearls, clams have a great impact in their own right on the eating habits of all of us.

The Quahogs are the backbone of clam eating. Their name, *Mercenaria mercenaria*, says money. And they produce plenty of it. But there are many other kinds that are eaten commercially. The Atlantic Surf Clam produces tons and tons of flesh for canned chowder. And the Soft-shell Clam alone furnishes us with raw food valued at more than $1,000,000 every year.

Those who work at digging these bivalves, those who buy and sell them, those who own the canning factories and the men and women who work in those factories, are completely dependent on these mollusks.

There are mussels and less well-known types of clams that are eaten in quantity, too. Each area has its local customs.

There are other bivalves that could be eaten if a person were fairly hungry. In most cases the reason they aren't is because they are very tough or hard to prepare or both. In Florida, for instance, the huge Quahog, *Mercenaria campechiensis*, is too tough to eat as is but makes a fine clam chowder when put through a meat grinder first.

There is much know-how and skill involved in digging Quahogs. They would be a lot more secure in their mud or sand hiding place if they wouldn't squirt a dead-giveaway jet of water into the air, though.

Clambakes have come to be a national institution. There are many methods, but all are based on a pit, rocks heated in the pit under a wood fire that burns a long time. Then finally the coals are raked off, the clams piled around the hot rocks, and wet seaweed banked over the whole. On an evening with a bright moon making a path across the water, a little singing, some side items (but most of the room saved for clams) you can get fairly close to Heaven on earth.

The catching and marketing of scallops is a huge industry. Scallops are a plentiful and delicious addition to the diet of those in seacoast areas and, with today's transportation, even those far from the sea. The thousands of persons engaged in the scallop industry are among those whose lives have been influenced by mollusks.

I have already described the way in which the Gooeyduck and the abalone are treated by West Coast residents more or less like wild game, and how rules and bag limits have been set for their taking. Here again many, many people depend on these for a money-saving entrée for their families.

Like these latter two mollusks, the conch of the West Indies provides many poor families with nourishing protein. Many a native who would otherwise have been hungry on a given night has eaten satisfyingly of conch, which cost him only the finding.

Even the Coquina makes delicious broth, and is not harsh in flavor like commercial clam broth. And this mollusk is, of all those I have so far mentioned, the least used because it is the least understood. Taking enough Coquinas for broth one by one is an endless task since they are so small. Sieving shovelfuls of sand from the waves' edge at mean tide gives the siever such a mass of dead shells along with his Coquinas that it is impossible to get good broth from this mess.

Yet there is a method for gathering Coquinas for broth which is simple, easy, foolproof. Few people know or use it. Yet with it you can get rid of all dead shells by simply taking advantage of the tiny mollusk's own behavior.

First off, your sieve can be a flat-bottomed affair with quarter-inch wire mesh if that is all you have. But if you are building one, it should look in side view like this:

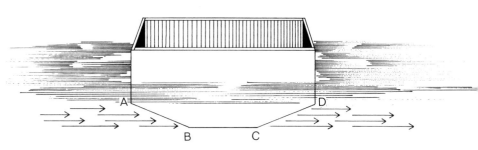

81. SIDE VIEW OF SIEVE. Sieve of quarter-inch mesh is attached to the bottom of this frame from point A through B to C and up to D. Thus the sieve rests only on the mesh base from B to C, leaving the mesh on the bottom between A and B and between C and D up off the beach. When the sieve is set near the water lengthwise (one narrow end toward the waves), each wave flows into the sieve through the mesh from A to B and out again from C to D, then recedes in the opposite direction and automatically washes the contents each time without the operator having to pick the sand and small bits of shell as he works.

Thus its weight does not rest on all the mesh, but only on a small section. If set on the beach lengthwise toward the water, each wave will wash through the mesh and do a lot of your sieving for you painlessly as you work.

You find the Coquinas by the tiny holes in the sand, myriads of them in a wavering line perhaps a yard wide along the beach. The longer the time between waves, and the more crowded the Coquinas are, the better the holes will show. When the sand is saturated with water, no holes show. Once you determine for yourself or are shown what the holes look like, you'll always recognize them. But you can test to make sure. Barefoot, worm your feet into the sand as a wave washes over the holes. The Coquinas, dislodged, will tumble along with the receding wave.

Now you know where they are for sure. You fill your sieve with your shovel or your dish or anything else that will do the job, and wash the resulting sieveful of material. When you think you have enough Coquinas mixed with the dead shells, you are ready for the cleaning step.

Empty your sieve into a pail or big kettle. Then fill the pail to within a couple of inches of the top with clean sand. Next add sea water (and be sure it gets through the sand down to the Coquinas) until the water is over the top of the sand by half an inch or an inch.

Next take the empty sieve and set it beside the pail on the beach. Kneel in front of the pail and with your hands stir the sand, the dead shells, the Coquinas and the water until you have everything in the pail loose and moving. When everything is liquid and in suspension, leave it alone for a few moments.

The dead shells during the stirring have sunk to the bottom of the pail, but the live Coquinas have come up to the top in a suspension of sand and water. Scoop this layer of pure Coquinas, sand and water off with your hands into the sieve beside the pail. When you think you have most of them, stir the whole mass again, adding water and sand to make up for what is gone. You'll get only a few this time.

In your sieve, after you wash what you now have, will be pure Coquinas for your broth. If you want to be amazed, dump what's left out of the pail and pour water on it to see the mass of dead shells you were able to get rid of. After the pail is again clean, dump the Coquinas into it, add sea water to cover. After a little while the mollusks will open, extend the foot and two siphons until the whole mass seems almost to have turned white. Left like this awhile, they will rid themselves of sand. But if you pour off the sea water and pour non-salt water on, instantly they will close for good and never open again, probably die. A Coquina broth recipe is given at the end of this chapter.

When you have made your broth the dish of Coquinas can be poked over, after it has cooled, and the most colorful double shells saved for your collection. You can flick out the animal with your fingernail and the shells can be spread like small butterflies on absorbent paper to dry.

All these mollusks we have talked about have exerted an influence for good. Yet there is one mollusk that has done millions and millions of dollar's worth of damage, has wasted human fortunes and is still wasting fabulous sums of money each year. We've already mentioned him; he is the shipworm. He honeycombs docks, dikes, wooden ships, anything wooden that lies for long in sea water. Huge timbers, perfect to outward appearance, suddenly crumble and let buildings fall. And when examined they are found to be a mass of calciumed holes with only an outside shell.

Steel vessels have been the salvation of the shipping industry. But still the shipworm continues to damage any wood he can lay his boring valves against. In the old days many of the ships that disappeared and left little trace could be chalked up indirectly to him.

So the molluscan impact is still tremendous. The picture has many heroes, some heroines. And one villain to end all villains.

OYSTER STEW
(*4 servings*)

1 pt. shucked oysters
½ stick butter (¼ cup)
1 qt. milk
1 cup light cream or evaporated milk
1 tsp. salt
1 tsp. paprika
2 tsp. Worcestershire sauce
A few drops Tabasco sauce

Look over the oysters for bits of shell. Drain but reserve the juice.

Melt butter over low heat in a heavy saucepan. Add the oysters and cook until oysters begin to curl.

Add the oyster juice, milk, cream and seasonings.

Heat to just under a boil and serve.

COQUINA BROTH

Pour away the sea water and swap the Coquinas from dish to dish to get rid of the sand they have expelled.

Then in the pot you'll use for cooking, put fresh water until it is about level with the top of the Coquinas; just a tiny bit under, if anything. Bring to a good boil.

The Coquinas will open wide with the heat. Pour off the broth. If you like things highly seasoned, add a little pepper. The salt from the juices retained inside the Coquinas will salt it enough. Serve as a clear hot broth.

19

The Great Shell-Collecting Areas of the World

THE extremely efficient barrier which holds the various species of mollusks each in its own area as completely as a wire fence could is water temperature. Actually it functions better than the finest-mesh fence, because the pelagic larvae of the oysters, for instance, could sift through any fence, grow and set up housekeeping on the far side.

The water-temperature barrier is like a pillow to mollusks; the farther they push into the temperature belt next to their own, the more trouble they have in penetrating still farther.

A few species are able to thrive in more than one temperature belt, and a very few thrive in all temperature belts either on their own or through subspecies. But mostly the water-temperature barrier is effective and holds them in their one belt.

The three major areas are the cold-water area, the temperate-water area and the warm-water area. These in turn are divided by continents, and are distorted by currents such as the Gulf Stream and the Japanese Current, which take warm waters far north to England and to Canada's British Columbia coast. There is, too, a vertical distortion in that species are sometimes found in shallow Arctic areas that are similar to others found in the near-freezing depths of some holes clear down in equatorial waters.

The cold-water area extends from the Arctic south along the European and American coasts in the Atlantic, and down the Asian and American coasts into the Pacific. At the opposite pole it touches the tip of South America and the south coast of Australia.

The temperate-water area, sometimes called the Carolinian Province on the East Coast and the California Province on the West Coast, extends from the Canadian border to Lower California, and from Cape Cod to Texas. But it does not extend all the way around Florida; the area roughly from St. Augustine on the east coast of Florida around the peninsula to Cedar Key on the west coast of Florida belongs in the warm-water area. Japan lies mostly in the temperate-water area and the part of Europe north of Portugal up to the Scandinavian peninsula does, too. Southern Africa belongs in this temperate area, from the rocky, storm-lashed tip up each coast to the level of the lower tip of Madagascar. Each coast of South America, up to Ecuador on one side and to Brazil on the other, has a strip of temperate water.

The warm waters of the world produce the greatest variety as well as the greatest numbers of interesting shells. The Caribbean area, including most of Florida and extending even part way down the coast of Brazil, has some 1,300 species. The larger islands of the West Indies, where food for mollusks is abundant, have almost all these species. The smaller ones have a third of them. From Lower California south to Ecuador on the other side of Central America, there are many of the West Indian species. This lends force to the theory that these two areas were once connected by water.

In the rest of the world, the most fabulous area of all is the area bounded on the west by the coast of Africa down to the southern tip of Madagascar, on the south by the northern coast of Australia, extending east to Easter Island and the Hawaiian group, and north to Japan. This whole vast area is alive with shelled mollusks, many, varied, interesting. There are literally thousands of tropical islands in this group. It includes the Philippines and the East Indies, the Marshalls, the Carolines, the Solomons.

Two nearly land-locked areas, the Red Sea and the Persian Gulf, border this main area and are connected to it. The Red Sea, probably because it is nearly land-locked, has many interesting variants of common warm-water shells.

In the warm-water area, too, is the nearly land-locked Mediterranean Sea, and the coasts at its western end which extend up to Spain and Portugal, and down to North Africa. I have already told you about the history-making Dye Murex and Jacob's Scallop from this warm-water area.

Within these subdivisions of the three basic temperature divisions there are several shell-gathering areas which are outstanding. It is impossible to say which of these is the best, for each offers a different type of shelling.

Then, to make a comparison even more difficult, the seasons enter in, the storm conditions, the growth and feeding cycles among the mollusks, and many other variants. For a few days after a hurricane I have known Sanibel Island to offer the finest shelling in the world. Three months later, after a long period of fine weather, it offered mediocre or even low-grade shelling. The Great Barrier Reef has sometimes been storm-lashed for weeks at a time so that no one could safely shell the reef itself. Here is another variant; the shells were undoubtedly there, but the shelling was nonexistent.

If for no other reason than its vast area and the diversity of its offerings, the Great Barrier Reef gets my nod as the overall, year-in and year-out best. Even in bad weather there are enough islands with lea beaches to offer fascinating hours and days of collecting if you can't shell the reef itself.

The problem here is distance. The reef is off the coast of Queensland, a state which comprises the whole northeast section of Australia. The Great Barrier stretches for a thousand miles or so and is thirty to sixty miles from the coast. The Capricorn Channel runs between the reef and the mainland.

In a channel of that width you can get fantastic waves, but they will not be the huge rollers of the ocean. They will be higher and narrower like the waves on North America's Great Lakes, or like the waves in the English Channel, to which this channel has been compared in its roughness. Obviously with those distances and that kind of waves, you need a big boat or good weather or both to get to good shelling.

First there is the island shelling. There are plenty of islands, but they are not the sand spits you would expect. They are wooded peaks, cliffs, very beautiful. On most of them you will find beaches where you can land and shell. The island itself provides protection for anchoring or landing. And some islands are known for the abundance of certain shells.

Island shelling here can be beach, shallow-water or deep-water. The main principles of these types of shelling apply just as they would anywhere.

Bowen, Queensland, Australia, is roughly opposite the middle of the reef and its citizens rent or charter boats and act as shell guides. Bowen is on the railroad, and can easily be reached from the major cities.

Shelling the reef itself is a major undertaking. The weather must be good and the tide conditions ideal for the expedition to be a success. You cross perhaps forty-five miles of what looks like open ocean, straight out away from land. While you are still in the middle of the ocean, as far as your own eyes tell you, your captain or guide drops anchor and you wait for low tide. The Great Barrier is a coral reef and soon the dark "heads" of dead coral begin to stick out of water. Shortly after that you can land from your dinghy on the reef, which will be awash.

To the shell collector and the marine scientist this is the ultimate. There are fascinating things growing, amazingly colored fish, mollusks, plants. Crabs are all colors. There are the Giant Clams sometimes, and the Giant Spider Crabs ten feet across their outspread claws. There is so much and such varied sea life that I cannot imagine a second trip duplicating the first trip to any great extent. The coral forms alone are fascinating. And you find many, many live shells.

In some ways it is a sobering experience to be wading ankle-deep and not to be able to see land in any direction. It is downright frightening when the tide has turned and started in, and you are knee-deep in a limitless ocean. Few shellers have to be called back to the boat more than once; the feeling of uneasiness is too strong inside them.

And remember there are miles of this stretching north and south. The molluscan inhabitants of one area differ radically from those of another, hundreds of miles distant; this is obvious when you consider the difference in cold and warmth which that many miles can make on our own continent. The prospects are limitless. Only money and time would keep a dedicated sheller from spending months and years moving from one interesting find to another.

The Philippine Islands group I rate next to the Barrier. Lying with its northern limits at about twenty degrees longitude and its southern limits close to the equator, it is ideally located to produce warm-water mollusks. It is, I hasten to add, no better located than the islands between Sumatra and New Guinea, or other areas of the Indo-Pacific Province. But it is at this writing safer for, and more accessible to, Americans and Europeans than many of the other islands.

And in the Philippines there are all the shells that anyone could want. Again the number of islands is so vast that all types of shelling can be found in the area. Like the Barrier, too, different islands are noted for different shells. There are beaches, there are flats, there is deep water and there is very deep water. Here again you have about a thousand miles of shell-producing area, each island different from the others and from the lonely, submerged Barrier Reef. But those combined islands offer shell collecting of at least equal interest.

There are other single islands or groups of islands in the world, other mainland beaches which might excel any spot in these two huge areas during any given month. Many of them are hard to reach and have no tourist facilities or charter facilities if you did reach them. Queensland, Australia, and the Philippines are both accessible and comfortable, and shelling arrangements are not hard to make at either.

Then in the United States there is Sanibel Island. I mention it again in spite of having already spoken of it so often because it is the best that we have here at home.

No fifteen-mile island and its surrounding waters can compare with a thousand miles of lonely reef or a thousand miles of assorted islands, year in and year out. But on a given day or a given week it could.

And Sanibel has accommodations that rank with the best. It has many cottage colonies, several motels, two hotels, and a causeway connecting it with the mainland so that you can drive directly to the beach you plan to shell. Several guides are available on Sanibel and neighboring Captiva who will take you shelling on the flats in their boats. Larger charter boats with the proper equipment can be chartered for dredging. Fine shell shops are located there. Or you can shell the beach or the flats on your own.

It has the shells, too. You will not find outstanding shells on the beach every day of the year, but after storms you will. There are many shells, even windrows of shells in some places, always. Anna Maria Key and Marco Island are somewhat like it.

The Great Barrier Reef and the Philippines and Tahiti and southern Japan are far, far places. And most of us have no money ever to reach them. But most of us do have cars and vacation time. And we can reach Anna Maria and Captiva and Sanibel. We can afford to stay there and shell there. And the shelling is as good as any fifteen-mile area anywhere.

20

Buying, Selling, Trading

SINCE it is true that most of us never have a chance to explore and to shell such places as the Great Barrier Reef and the Philippines, our only chance at shells from far places comes through purchase or trade. Fortunately, people who live in these far places consider us as living in far places, too. Many of them are just as anxious for our shells as we are for theirs, and therefore want to trade. Others make or supplement their living by finding and selling the shells of their areas. Everybody benefits.

Buying is most easily accomplished through a dealer. In rare cases it may be possible to deal directly with the finder, especially with very valuable shells. News spreads rapidly among shell collectors that So-and-So found a perfect Prince Cowrie. It is available and he is holding it for the best offer.

But with ordinary shells, you and the finder have little opportunity to know about each other. He sells to a dealer; you have access to the dealer or to his lists. If you visit his place of business you have a chance to examine the shell before you pay for it. You know what you are getting.

How do you find a dealer? First look in the yellow pages of your telephone directory. In many large cities—New York, Chicago, Los Angeles, Philadelphia—this will give you either the name and phone number of a dealer, or it will give you the phone number of a shell club. A call to the shell club will usually get the nearest dealer's name.

But suppose this doesn't work; what then?

The American Malacological Union, Inc., founded in 1931, puts out a list of dealers. If you plan on collecting shells, my advice would be to join the Malacological Union. It is "dedicated to the study and appreciation of mollusks and their shells." And it "cordially invites all interested persons to affiliation." The dues at this writing are $3 a year for residents of the United States and Canada, an extra $.50 where postal rates are higher. There is an annual meeting, usually at a large university or museum, and the Pacific Coast division has its own annual meeting to cut the cost of attendance for members from states which are far from eastern centers.

In addition to the list of dealers, the Union puts out a list of members and their "special malacological interests." This list is sent with the annual-meeting report to all members. The Union also has available a list of "Shell Clubs Around the World." Most of these are affiliated with the Union. You may find that there is one of these clubs within traveling distance of the area in which you live or in which you shell. The address of the A.M.U. is: The American Malacological Union, Margaret C. Teskey, Secretary, Route 2, Box 318, Marinette, Wisconsin, 54143.

Another gold mine of information is a booklet called "Sources of Information on Mollusks" put out by the Division of Mollusks, U. S. National Museum, Washington, D.C. This is available without cost.

A magazine called *Johnsonia* has been published since the early 1940s by William J. Clench, Museum of Comparative Zoology, Cambridge, Massachusetts. It is highly thought of and is for the advanced sheller.

If you plan to buy shells, how can you be sure the price asked is a fair one?

Many dealers prepare price lists of specimen shells. Comparing several of these lists will give you a price consensus for the shell you are interested in obtaining. And the first edition of *Van Nostrand's Standard Catalog of Shells* gives values for almost all known cones, cowries, volutes, vases, slit shells, conchs and a few other outstanding shells. The publishers say that in later editions they plan to include more groups. If the shell you covet is in one of these groups, looking it up in *Van Nostrand's Catalog* would give you price advice.

If you scorn buying or haven't the money to purchase what you want, trading with other shell collectors all over the world may be the answer. If you have a lot of specimens of the semi-rare shells of your area and a few duplicates of the rare ones, you might be able to put together with patience and effort a very fine collection of far-places shells just by trading.

How do you go about it?

First you need a list of all the conchologists throughout the world who are eager to trade with other shell collectors. For a great many years Mr. John Q. Burch of 4206 Halldale Avenue, Los Angeles, California, sold such a mimeographed list. This list became for most traders their standard tool. Within a few months of the time this is being written, Mr. Burch has retired and sold out. From now on he will handle only in-print and out-of-print books "on shells and other natural history subjects." His is a fantastic list of out-of-print shell books, some of which are valued in the hundreds of dollars.

The "Directory of Conchologists" which Mr. Burch for so many years published for traders is to be published hereafter by Mr. Richard Petit, P. O. Box 133, Ocean Drive Beach, South Carolina, 29582. The price is $3.

So the directory will continue to be available and a copy of it not only will give the trader the names he needs, but also will indicate the types of shells in which each listed person is most interested. This is done with symbols in letters and numbers after each name and address.

In a foreword Mr. Petit says, "Although this edition is very small, it should be very useful as all information is current." "Small" most certainly is relative; the rough count I made showed around 1,100 names listed from all over the world. Mr. Petit also says that the supplement which he will bring out later may very well contain as many additional names as there are names in the original edition. This would bring the total up over 2,000.

Florida and California have the most names among the states. The representation of some twenty names from Hawaii should be most interesting to continental collectors; these people undoubtedly have shells which are not available to the rest of us. Puerto Rico, the Virgin Islands and the Canal Zone also are represented.

In the listings outside the United States there are eighty names from Australia. I noticed several names from Queensland, which is Great Barrier Reef territory, even two from Bowen, which I spoke of in the previous chapter. There are nine names from the Philippines and five from Japan.

There are conchologists from Africa, the Canary Islands, Greece, Malta, Israel, New Guinea (Bougainville Island), Tahiti, and under a listing of "Pacific Islands (Miscellaneous)," two names.

Uruguay has a large listing and, believe it or not, the U.S.S.R. has eight entries and Hungary has four.

In addition to these, there are all the large countries which you would expect to be listed as well as other fascinating and little-known places. In all there are forty-nine countries listed besides the United States, including Iceland and Fiji.

There are, then, a wealth of people who are interested enough in trading to fill out a questionnaire and allow themselves to be a part of this directory.

Once you have names, you establish contact by letter. If an agreement is reached, you ship the promised shells. Sometimes the agreement is very definite. Sometimes it is loose— a promise only to send a representative selection. The other person, when he is in receipt of these, sends *his* selection in return, roughly at about the same valuation. Use only Latin names.

Sometimes under such a system you get cheated, so it is

best to start in a small way until you see how matters go. There have been cases where, in return for a rather good selection, the sender received a poorly packed pile of beach-worn, unlabeled specimens. This is a risk you take; at least you never need trade with that person again.

But most people bend over backward to give full value. They pack carefully, label clearly and fully. And they send specimens which the other person can be proud to own. Always exactly state (even understate) the condition of the shells you want to trade rather than overstate it. If, for instance you have filed the uneven lip of a shell, be sure to say so. If you do this, the recipient will want to trade with you again.

As your collection grows you will gradually move from shotgun-type trading to rifle-type trading. Instead of a selection from a certain area you will trade for one specific shell which you are anxious to acquire.

When you trade, the shells you are furnishing must arrive at their destination in perfect condition. This is not always easy to accomplish if your package happens to come in contact with one of the comparatively few forwarders who are heavy-handed and don't intend to change. Since there are such people, your package and your packing must be proof against their ministrations.

Pick a good heavy cardboard carton, one that has not already been damaged. Line the bottom with crumpled, pressed-down newspapers. These make a shock-resistant bed for whatever you plan to send.

If you have tiny shells, pack them with tissue or cotton batting in small medicine vials or tiny boxes. If they are small (but not tiny) shells, pack them with cotton or crumpled tissue in candy boxes or even cigar boxes. Large shells can be packed loose in the carton without too much danger of damage if you give them enough padding.

Line the sides of your carton with more crumpled newspapers and place your vials or boxes on the bottom bed of newspapers. If you are packing large shells, too, insulate them from the boxes and any other large shells by more crumpled newspapers.

Each layer should be insulated in this way from the layer above and below, and from the sides of the carton. Don't be afraid to press the crumpled papers in hard; if you have packed them hard they won't be likely to pack down in transit and allow everything inside the carton to shuck around.

On top, place a final layer of crumpled newspaper, enough so that you have to press down hard on the cover to hold it in place. Tie the package securely, label carefully and clearly, printing the address in crayon or some other material which will not run if the package should be transferred from vehicle to vehicle in the rain.

Nothing is proof against a determined package-wrecker. But this packing will come as close as you can get. Be naïve and hopeful, and mark the thing FRAGILE.

Trading will actually furnish you more then shells. It will put you in correspondence with people who have the same interests you have, in remote areas of the globe. If you treat them well, some of them will trade with you over and over and perhaps become your friends. I have known of cases where shell collectors on a world tour have looked up people with whom they had become acquainted only through shell trading.

This, then, is shell collecting. It is a hobby that stimulates interest and learning. It opens the doors of travel and friendship, of exercise and health.

I hope you will enjoy your collecting to the utmost and will pass from your earlier efforts, through which this book has led you, on to more sophisticated and more specialized shelling.

May your efforts be blessed always with many, many Junonias.

Glossary

Acid—a chemical used for cleaning the outside of shells.

Adductor muscle—the bivalve muscle used to hold the two valves closed.

Albinos—pure-white specimens of nonwhite shells.

Anterior canal—lower canal, where there are two.

Anterior end—forward end of a bivalve.

Aperture—the opening of a univalve shell.

Apex—tip, or beginning point, of a snail mollusk.

Author—the scientist who first discovers and names a mollusk.

Base—a chemical, usually a salt, used for neutralizing an acid.

Beak—the beginning point of a bivalve.

Bivalve—an animal which has two valves hitched together by a ligament.

Body Whorl—the open last whorl, usually containing most of the body.

Byssus—threadlike filaments used by bivalves to attach themselves to something.

Canal—a groove in the aperture of a univalve.

Canal notch—the canal opening as seen from the outside.

Carnivorous—flesh-eating.

Columella—the center of a univalve shell around which the animal's body is curled.

Conchologist—a student of shells.

Crustaceans—aquatic anthropods usually having a thin, brittle covering for the body; not mollusks.

Cubit—unit of measurement for wampum; elbow to tip of little finger.

Dextral—right-handed.

Dredging—a method of bringing up deep-water shelled mollusks.

Ears—*see* wings.

Egg cases—various-shaped, strung-together containers made of tough, plasticlike material, in which some mollusks lay their eggs.

Extrude—to push outside (the body).

Eye stalk—stalks growing from the bodies of some mollusks, the ends of which contain each an eye.

Fecundity—fertility.

Foot—a molluscan organ usually used for locomotion or digging.

Fossils—shells of past geological eras.

Free pearl—a pearl formed completely within the mantle.

Generic name—the first word in a mollusk's Latin name.

Gill—a molluscan organ sometimes used in eating as well as breathing.

Growth rings—the thickened lip at the end of each growth stage on which the next stage is built.

Gunwale—the top rim of the sides of a small boat.

Herbivorous—plant-eating.

Hinge—area of joining of the valves of a bivalve.

Inner lip—part of the columella.

Larva—in some mollusks the stage following the hatching of the egg.

Ligament—cartilage which holds the two valves of a bivalve together. .

Lip—rim of the mouth.

Lunule—a depressed spot in front of the beaks in many bivalves.

Malacologist—a student of mollusks.

Mammalian—having to do with mammals.

Mangrove—a tropical bushlike tree which puts down leafless feelers into the water.

Mantle—molluscan body part which manufactures the shell.

Miniatures—tiny specimens of shells.

Minus tide—extra low tide occurring when sun and moon exert their pull in the same line.

Mopping—a process of bringing to the surface mollusks and starfish.

Mother-of-pearl—the irridescent inside of a shell.

Mouth—*see* aperture.

Mucus—a viscid, slippery secretion.

Nacre—the iridescent material with which the inside of shells is made.

Nodules—nubs.

Nurse eggs—eggs in the capsules of egg cases which seem to be not for hatching, but for the nourishment of the young.

Operculum—fingernaillike substance on the end of the foot of many univalves used to close the opening.

Orient—flamelike luster in a pearl.

Pallial line—a line paralleling the inner lip of a bivalve and made by the muscle edge of the mantle.

Parasite—mollusks which live within other creatures and take all nourishment from them.

Pelagic—free-swimming.

Periostracum—a soft growth covering the outside of many shells.

Phyla—the largest divisions of the animal world, the mullusks constitute one phylum.

Posterior canal—upper canal, where there are two.

Posterior end—back end of a bivalve.

Predator—an animal preying on other animals.

Proboscis—molluscan organ mainly used in feeding.

Radula ribbon—a ribbon of teeth in the proboscis.

Resilium—internal cartilage which causes a bivalve to open when not held together by the adductor muscle.

Shell—the hard calcium structure produced by a mollusk, usually as a body covering.

Sinistral—left-handed.

Siphon—a molluscan organ through which water enters the body.

Skate—a batlike fish of the ray family.

Snout—*see* proboscis.

Spat—young of some mollusks, notably oysters, in their pelagic period.

Specific name—the second word in a mollusk's Latin name, which distinguishes it from others of that genus.

Spire—the whorls above the body whorl in a univalve.

Stinger—the harpoonlike needle in the proboscis connected with a poison sack.

Subspecific name—the third word in a four-word Latin name.

Sutures—the lines of the joining of one whorl to another.

Tangle—a gathering of cord pieces designed to be dragged along the ocean bottom.

Tentacles—long wormlike or snakelike feelers.

Tide table—a forecast of tide times for a given area.

Tyrian purple—a dye made from the murex, a status symbol of olden times.

Umbo—the beginning part of a bivalve as it emerges from the egg; usually points forward.

Univalves—a mollusk having only one valve.

Valve—a shell complete in itself.

Wampum—processed shells or pieces of shell strung and used for money.

Wings—extensions of the hinge area in bivalves such as pectens.

Whorl—each turn of the univalve shell around the columella.

Selected Bibliography

Abbott, R. Tucker, *American Seashells*. D. Van Nostrand Co., Inc., 1954.

Abbott, R. Tucker, *Sea Shells of the World*. Golden Press, Inc., 1962.

Aldrich, Bertha D. E. and Snyder, Ethel, *Florida Sea Shells*. Houghton Mifflin Co., 1936.

Allen, Joyce, *Australian Shells*. Georgian House, 1950.

Bevans, Michael H., *The Book of Sea Shells*. Doubleday & Co., Inc., 1961.

Cameron, Roderick, *Shells*. G. P. Putnam's Sons, 1961.

Clemons, Elizabeth, *Tidepools and Beaches*. Alfred A. Knopf, Inc., 1964.

Dance, S. Peter, *Shell Collecting: An Illustrated History*. University of California Press, 1966.

Habe, Tadashige, *Shells of the Western Pacific*, Vol. II. Hoikusha Publication Co., 1962.

Johnstone, Kathleen Yerger, *Sea Treasure*. Houghton Mifflin Co., 1956.

Kira, Tetsuski, *Shells of the Western Pacific*, Vol 1. Hoikusha Publication Co., 1962.

Melvin, A. Gordon, *Sea Shells of the World with Values*. Charles E. Tuttle Co., 1966.

Morris, Percy A., *Field Guide to the Shells of Our Atlantic and Gulf Coast*, rev. ed. Houghton Mifflin Co., 1951.

Morris, Percy A., *Field Guide to the Shells of the Pacific Coast and Hawaii*. Houghton Mifflin Co., 1952.

Verrill, A. Hyatt, *Shell Collector's Handbook*. G. P. Putnam's Sons, 1950.

Wagner, Robert J. L. and Abbott, R. Tucker, *Van Nostrand's Standard Catalog of Shells*, 2 vols. D. Van Nostrand Co., 1964.

Webb, Walter Freeman, *Handbook for Shell Collectors*, 16th rev. ed. Lee Publications, 1948.

Index